AquaPyro Dynamics
(Physics of Good & Evil)

by Ron Gates

Published by EARTHOVISION Publishing
Valley Glen, California
For more information please visit
www.AquaPyro.com or www.EARTHOVISION.com

ISBN: 978-1-943823-02-4
Library of Congress Control Number: 2015948541
Printed in the United States of America
First Edition and First Printing: MMXV

INTRODUCTION

Humans have brewed and developed for a long time, and you now find yourselves in the awkward position of passing from one stage into another. Just as humans matured from animal to toolmaker and from tribes to civilizations, you are again taking another step forward. Years ago humans moved from the medieval era of violence and destruction to the renaissance era with peace and creation. You will now move into an era of advanced power with an understanding of yourselves in relation to the real physical world, and the worlds in your minds.

Both inside and outside yourselves are creative, watery forces, and destructive, fiery forces. These outside forces become a part of who you are on the inside. When you favor one side over the other, you become good or bad, creative or destructive, you become Aquaian or Pyroian.

You are about to travel deep into the mysteries of yourself and the life around you. In the course of your study here you will learn to organize the complex world around you into a nice, neat package and then move deeper into the powers that make all the magic happen in the first place. You are about to become a proud, powerful human with a solid foundation and understanding of life's basics including your place here, and what is expected of you in return.

There are times where you'll catch yourself maturing before your own eyes and what was important in your old life is replaced by more intelligent directions and endeavors for your new life. The difference between your constructive side and your destructive side is not hard to understand. The fiery nature that gets you into trouble and the watery nature that brings you peace are both available for you to choose.

Do you have an Aquaian mindset or a Pyroian mindset? Are you happy with your mindset so far? The more you understand these two sides of yourself the better you can choose which one to give priority to.

CHAPTERS

Bridal Veil Falls (Oil on canvas) by Albert Bierstadt (1871)

Chapter 1
SURVIVAL

As you officially begin your study here let's use your imagination to travel back to one of the important scenes in mankind's story; the point where he matured from a created animal to a creating animal.

It's an amazing position the human finds himself in, to be suspended somewhere between animal and God, the created, and the Creator. This point in man's development made possible his rising above the thoughts of a mortal's mind to the thoughts of the Creator's mind.

Before this transcendence occurred, man's ancestors spent their days very differently compared to your current activities. Back then they lived, not in a man-made world, but in nature's world, where animals spend their entire day, in the harmonious drama of survival.

Most of this time was needed to collect food and the time left over was devoted to survival in other forms of activity such as; avoiding becoming food, grooming the parasites off their bodies, elimination of the things they had eaten & drank, reproduction activities, and other physical drives important to long term survival.

To also better their survival skills they practiced

motor activities. The connections between the mind, the body, and the movement that results. An example is when a child learns to walk. At first the body may seem clumsy, but soon the motor activities develop and the body may move with more elegance and integrated abilities.

It was "survival" that governed development up until then and the time has arrived to create a new goal to strive for. This new turning point is needed because the human's motor skills, physical body, and mind have developed past the point needed for the basic survival activities. He has slowly become ultra-efficient.

During this progression, man was able to obtain his items of survival in less time, and thus was left with free time during the day to just sit and observe the world before him. This free-thinking continued to grow, as he was able to observe his mind juggling the images collected in the past with the images he was now sensing. He kept enlarging and strengthening his mind through these extracurricular activities, these daydreams. He took pieces apart, and replaced pieces with different pieces. He put things together to create things not found or thought before.

It's this man, lying under a tree, thinking about the animal he just caught, that creates in his head a better way to catch the animal next time. He has broken out of a type of slavery from where his life is controlled by instinct or higher forces to an ability to create and control his own life, his own actions, and reactions.

Asleep in the Wood (Oil on canvas) by Arthur Hughes (1832-1915)

From here, mankind continued to better his survival actions through envisioning better tools, ways of using the tools, herding their prey into corrals, and cultivating the plant life by collecting seeds and planting, etc.. Still further down the road, humans were creating more complicated things from plant, animal, and mineral life such as shelters, clothes, and more advanced tools. Don't forget now, the more efficient he becomes, the more idle time he has left over in the day to spend in the mind.

This mental world that humans visit keeps growing and it's this mental world that all humans must now confront. The goal from the beginning has been for survival, and long ago this was more than met. Physically, humans are at the top of the animal world totem pole, and the ease with which they gather life's necessities make survival no longer the struggle it used to be.

Humans are left with a need to create a new goal for their minds to accomplish. This cannot be ignored as it has been up to now or mankind will continue struggling to survive even if he must create the struggle in his own head.

All his economic dangers, struggles to avoid these dangers, mazes in their lives, jungles in their minds, things they just must do, dollars they just must make, and so called needs for their survival are really all in the head, made up in man's mental world. That original striving towards survival such as for food, shelter, and security were accomplished by man's ingenuity long ago and he was left with a mental dilemma where to get the necessities of life one must survive in a man-made, economic environment.

A truly advanced society has its food and shelter figured out. It is taken for granted that the combined intelligence and efforts of the people will achieve the basics of survival for its members like water, food, and shelter with less effort than if done independently. This is why they would bother to be a part of a community in the first place, for the benefits of combined efforts.

So what happens to the instinct of survival? The next big step in humans maturing requires that you learn to survive, not simply in the physical world, but now, in the mental world which can be even more complicated and tricky. With all this free time you are going to have to keep yourself occupied, and what else have you other than your imagination and creativity to explore? This is where you spend your free time anyway. When you make this your new driving force the simple survival needs will no longer be a struggle. The struggle now is to strengthen your mind to survive efficiently in your free time.

Chapter 2
FREE TIME

One ironic drawback in mankind's history was marked when he invented factories and machines to mass produce his food and other items. Now instead of people, there were machines that spent their day making the things needed in human lives. This didn't leave humans much to do in the way of taking care of their own needs and they ended up keeping occupied with unrealistic jobs such as sitting at desks, shuffling paperwork back and forth, collecting and spending money, and doing math.

Kings and rulers have known for a long time that if people are given too much freedom and not kept occupied that this "idleness leads to devil's work". People with no direction in life fall into a type of craziness. So the current folks that design the blueprints of your societies always keep humans busy. Even if it's just dealing with numbers, words, forms or other jobs that are in actuality of no benefit to the real physical world.

But this leads to frustration, and a society of unhappy people. The creative potential in each person has no limits and to stifle one's activities in this world of wonder can be very frustrating. Many think that they hate their work, and would like to never work again, but really it's the repetition and boredom that they hate. If their wish was granted and they could just sit there and do nothing eventually they would become fidgety and get up to join the others.

Market Day (Oil on canvas) Nicolai Francois Habbe (1867-1928)

It's a deep need to be a part of what's going on, to be with others, to get your hands into your life and the world around you. This basic need is what is used by the blueprint designers of your societies. They know you will join in no matter what's happening or how crazy and unfair the system is. Humans must have some sort of blueprint that shows how they all fit together. As history shows it can be any blueprint no matter how flawed, and there is no ultimate blueprint invented so far.

So setting current, outdated societies aside you find that even in an advanced society, filled with freedom, there are still basic common directions and goals. All those goals beyond physical survival are mainly how you spend your extra free time in well thought out, productive directions.

Before you are ready to play with your concept of free time we should make sure your foundation of basic survival understanding has solidified, and is firmly in place. The average, or even above-average, person may have been surviving in the man-made world (with lots of money and interesting possessions,) but drop him in the world of reality (forest, jungle, desert, etc.,) and most could not survive. Even the plants and animals, that man would consider beneath him, knew more about taking care of themselves and survival in reality.

Man didn't know such basics as what plants and other foods were edible and would starve unless someone else did it for him. Man didn't have the knowledge to build his own shelter as many animals can do. His mating skills and family habits were so man-made that many dramas unfolded with unnatural results such as anger, frustration, and traumatized children. Man had moved so far from the basics which sustain life that even when he pronounced himself the smartest thing around, in reality he was really very pitiful and just didn't know that much.

So if mankind wants to brag about being such a big deal he is going to have to learn a lot more than just how to count and spell. Out of all the animal languages and ways of communicating, how many does he understand? From the many plants that grow around him, which ones can he eat and which ones are poisonous? An advanced human should know how to fasten together wood to make a chair, cotton fibers to make clothes, and ceramic mud to make one's own eating bowl.

Since humans are going to have so much free time you might as well find more ways to spend some of that time taking care of your own needs. Give the machines a break, or let them handle the math and paperwork. Using your own hands to make the items in your lives is rewarding and is also a very good use of all that free time you must fill.

An advanced human learns how to harvest his meals, make his clothes, build a home, create a table, and even how to make his own snowshoes. If everyone used snowshoes that they themselves made, humans would have a very interesting variety of snowshoes. Then the chances for new innovative designs would go up, and these designs would keep getting better and more efficient. Notice how these new designs tantalize and inspire those that see them. Notice how the world also becomes that much more complex, detailed, interesting and improved.

A man poor in his abilities would have to trade money for something so amazing, but a man rich in abilities and with true creative power can figure out how to make his own, and sometimes make it even better. The elite now are not represented by how much money they have, or power over others, but by the mental power over themselves to create amazing things, and it's this that gains a deeper admiration from those other people around them.

Now, a power trip is not seen as dominance and ruling over others, but the power he has matured inside himself. This kind of power trip is seen by others and it's this that inspires them to follow this creative person's direction. To admire other people's creative powers pushes you from pleasant bedazzlement to learning the secrets of how it works.

When an advanced human sees that someone has an amazing item of ingenuity, such as a moving sculpture, he doesn't want to buy it. Instead he examines the levers, positions of the gears and wheels until he has the power to recreate the sculpture. A Pyroian tries to impress his family and friends with how much money he has and things he has bought. An Aquaian impresses others with examples of his power as a creative being and things he has made.

Everything you do and create in the real world is an example of you. It represents you. The hat that you make and wear represents your abilities and creative power levels of hat building. You may walk up to someone and tell them your name, but your name does not represent your true self as well as the clothes you made for yourself or the new piece of art you created.

Since you change every day with new experiences, ways of seeing life, and creative abilities, how can you conform to only one name forever? Turn things around and examine the person that keeps changing, growing and opens their mind to becoming a better person.

How often do you think about your name and the fact that from your birth it is used to represent you, for the rest of your life, yet you didn't create this symbol that represents you? Who you are is not chiseled in stone forever, and because who you are changes, so should what represents who you are. This holds true for your society in general. The blueprint that dictates how you spend the day is also not set in stone. Neither is what you name yourselves as a country, state, or town.

Once a country lets go of old, bad habits and lets itself change in dramatic ways, it is on the same maturing path that its people are traveling. Without the ability to let go and move forward, you will find stagnation and frustration. To spend all one's time examining history and using this information as a foundation leads to a shaky system.

The problems are continually mended with bandages, yet the flawed, original cores continue to be flawed. If you try to dictate that someone not do something and they break the law then the law is flawed and doesn't work. If a law is broken, it can't be fixed, because it was too old or wasn't built right in the first place. Or the overall book of laws don't sit well and leave the citizens frustrated. Like the laws of physics, the laws that a human holds in his mind must ring true. Outside force is not needed for true laws (they come from the inside.)

Up until now the goal has been to create better people and safer civilizations. The past is full of mistakes, barbaric scenes, and unjust laws, and it's the past that humans are trying to rise above. Let go of the bumbling attempts through history and create something new. If you are to get some momentum towards your advanced future you have to stop looking backwards. Let go of your flawed history and put your attention in the opposite direction. Turn around a full 180 degrees and face the future.

A creative artist wastes their time painting what's already here. You might as well take a picture. You may see something upsetting in the world but painting tragic and upsetting scenes doesn't help. Showing what you don't like makes things worse. Everyone can already see the things they don't like and you don't need to add even more to all the negative stuff seen. The whole point of being creative is to create something new.

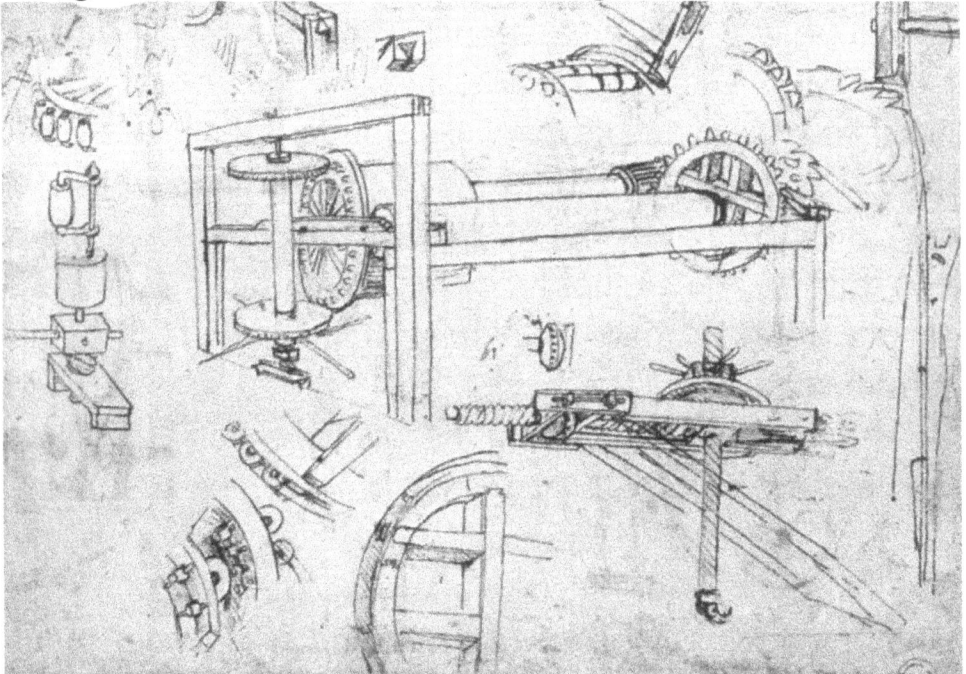

Sketch by Leonardo da Vinci (1452-1519)

Create something beyond what was here before. If something seems wrong to an artist it's up to them to create an advanced vision. Create something better. If something positive inspires you don't just duplicate it. Create something even better.

Create something more refined. Don't waste time painting what you don't like about the world. Spend your time painting what you would like.

Soon countries will be as colorfully decorated as the humans that comprise them. Each citizen a proud ornament worn to represent how creative a country is. Each citizen has designed many items in their lives and is as unique as a fingerprint.

Imagine if everyone did actually design their own clothes, tools, homes, public spaces, ornaments, and entertainment. What a complex, beautiful world that would be, and your minds would eat this up like candy. Your brains chew on information all day and the same old diet can get monotonous. Throw in something new and watch how your brain happily starts churning.

So if you take some of your free time and use it for your survival time, beyond the food and water needs into needs such as clothes, and tools, then you will spend more time in the real physical world. This will help you to better appreciate and respect this real world. With this solid tether to reality, the human, with all his free time, can then dive into the infinite vastness of creativity and not get lost.

Chapter 3
CREATIVITY

This topic can get very deep and complicated so let's create a simple formula to start from. Creativity is a process that occurs when one thing is added with a second thing, and thus born is a third thing. Something new and more complex than the first two.

It's through this basic yet powerful creative process that everything has been built up so far, both in the physical world, and the mental world. Humans find this all through the universe and this simple formula even answers basic questions such as, "What is your shadow?" When light is mixed with matter, thus born is a shadow. When elements and compounds come together, thus born are molecules. When these then come together you get bio-forms, until so many things come together, and then you get that complicated thing like a seed, a rabbit, or a dinosaur. From all the things humans marvel at, deep down, it's yourselves that really make you wonder.

Creativity is a word that can be used to answer most of man's questions. Normally, it would be God that would be responsible for all the magic going on and the unexplained phenomena around you, but notice that God can also be called the Creator. The one behind making the amazing animals, plants, and lightning storms. The one responsible for everything you find around you.

We will examine God as a being in a later chapter, but for now let's limit your study of God to the accomplishments and activities that are right here in front of you, in your abilities to understand and comprehend.

It's all of these creative pieces in this museum that humans admire anyway. It's this fully developed mastery of creative power that humans praise the ultimate Creator. Just as you may never meet the body of Michelangelo, you can still admire his creative mind by the paintings and sculptures he has created (and you'll wish you could make such amazing things as well.)

The Creation of Adam (Fresco Painting) by Michelangelo (1510)

Learning to understand and strengthen your powers of creativity will bring you closer to understanding the mind of God, so if you ever get to meet him at least you'll understand his language. All humans have creative abilities, but many haven't used or practiced their talents. Typical jobs have limited their growth to narrow directions, and their chances to excel have been very stifled. Most jobs don't benefit the real physical world so they are a waste of time.

In an advanced society, the members have many talents and expressions of their creativity to share with the other members. Once the dwellings have been built and the water systems organized, those that will most benefit the others in their society, are those that use their minds and personal powers to surpass the known. To create things that completely dazzle those that see them.

We all love to see new and exciting things. Your brains absorb the world around you and can get bored with the same old menu. When your brain sees a spectacle, or something new, it goes to work chewing and digesting. So you all must take turns as audience and performer. Just as you admire other creations, you must also create pieces to share and inspire. Those that love to read books will only complete the circle when they have written a book. You can hear wonderful music, and be inspired to make music. The same with poetry, sculpture, landscaping, art, making movies, and a multitude of results that show your advancing levels of creativity.

This is where you will find importance and truer reasons to be admired by those around you. This is where you find true acceptance and well-being, knowing you are a part of the magic around you, and others can see high or low levels of it in you. You now have a meaningful connection between that deep, special, individual inside you to the other special individuals that you dwell with.

Let's practice your creativity on deeper questions from your psyche. "Why am I alive?" is left unanswered until one actually *creates* reasons to be alive. You get to figure out what you will do with your life, what you will make, and how you will make it. "Who am I?" is easy to answer when you know that you're a creative being who keeps maturing and changing, and it's the accomplishments from your creative hands that represent who you are. The "I" in question is the part of you that is individual, or beyond the you that has been absorbed from outside the self. It is from the inside out, and it makes each of you unique and special. The creative "I."

For years there were questions such as, "What is the ultimate experience?" and "What is the ultimate state of being?" When you examine the life of an artist you will find that while emerged in one's work, a deep state is induced. It is peaceful, harmonic, and closer to God. All true artists can tell you that while creating something, you can lose yourself in a trance-like state, a bliss if you will. The artist's ego disappears and the creative force flows through them.

The Artists Studio (Oil on canvas) by Pierre Jules Jollivet (1794-1871)

Upon regaining consciousness, and seeing what was created, an artist will feel they were really only a tool for a bigger, more intelligent Creator. This is one of the closest experiences of God's mental state a simple human can obtain.

The bliss experienced during free flowing creativity can also be compared to the sexual climax. One's ego melts away and the conscious self is as if drugged or in a dreamland. Needless to say we've arrived back at the definition of creativity; one person plus a second person equals a whole new third person (you can study sex from top to bottom and still be left with the facts such as the actual outcome, the child. There in the outcome is the simple reason for this complicated topic of two coming together; sex. More on this topic later.)

In the real, physical world you can create many amazing things, but to create another human is the highest expression of your abilities, yet the knowledge is beyond human understanding. Humans couldn't consciously tell you how to make a butterfly much less the blueprint on how to make a human baby, and in fact your conscious minds were scrambled at the time of actual conception (or at least the orgasm.) You can't take the credit for this ultimate creative ability to make more of yourselves. Your creator gets this credit. As far as your conscious minds are concerned, it is the loophole to avoid the death of the species. It propels what makes humans special beyond the short, individual life spans.

The old concept of reincarnation was attempting to grasp life beyond death, but let's break things down again from the beginning with a new, advanced perspective. In the physical world humans can reproduce their physical bodies in the form of children, and although they die, the children will live on to repeat the process. A separate world is the mental world, and for your minds to live on you must understand the difference between your mental world and your physical world.

The concepts of reincarnation are scrambled until you realize that the "you" that you want to live on is the thinking you in your head. It's the you with your name, memories, and sense of self. The multitude of thoughts that you have arranged to comprise who you are, in your head, is quite different from the physical body "you."

When the body dies it decomposes and the physical, tangible cells live on, being absorbed into other life-form endeavors like plants, and then into little rabbits, and then into dinosaurs and such. When you hear about a body decomposing, remind yourself about the following stage of recomposing. Things break down into their smaller pieces, but then these smaller pieces are used to rebuild up bigger things. Each cell has a new life to live. Your cells eaten by a worm now live in the worm. When it dies, the plant's roots suck up its pieces and they end up in leaves. A deer comes along, eats the leaves, and these small pieces of you are now in a deer, and so on.

Just as your physical body doesn't disappear but is used in future endeavors, so does the mind live on, but only if absorbed into other peoples heads or in physical creations. The most interesting parts of yourself are the ones that you yourself created; they're original and set differently than any of the others.

All history is filled with people that created something new, and long after they had died their creativity, that went beyond what was already created, is what lived on.

Ludwig van Beethoven (Painting) by Joseph Karl Stiele (1820)

Beethoven may have died long ago but his music is still alive. His head was comprised of words and thoughts that were around before he was born just as you all go through a growing stage of absorbing everything created so far.

When Beethoven started creating something that wasn't there before, he latched onto the powerful creative force, and his special, unique, mental spirit emerged and lived on after his physical body died. His individual self, even his name, managed to get into the mental world humans all share where it grew and flourished. He's still alive today, there in your head.

Up to this point human minds have been filled with outside influences created by others, words created by others, religions and laws created by others. It's a mental world that's been added to for thousands of years. This mental world filled with items from long ago is still growing, and is added to by those that explore their creative abilities. It's the mental world that you all share in common, and it holds you together. It connects your minds despite the emptiness, or air, between you.

From outside yourselves you've absorbed languages, styles, expressions, understandings, dress habits and ways of dealing with people. When these masses of thoughts are in two individual heads, the two heads are now connected as one. They both vibrate similar intricate patterns that harmonize with the other. They share one mind.

This is one of the magical attributes of your lives that you must understand and then incorporate this understanding into your common belief systems. If the YOU, with your name, never creates something new to add, then all that makes YOU will still live on past your death. But these thoughts and words that make YOU were around before you were born. It's better to leave something new behind to show for all your trouble. The life span of a human requires a lot of input like food and water, so if you don't get creative the only thing you will output will end up in the sewer. You're capable of more than that.

The physical world is an amazing land to be in which also itself was created by the power of creation. But the mental world is ever so much larger and powerful. In the physical world humans are bound and connected by an invisible, magical space. A person may connect to, and accomplish an awareness of other items or beings outside their self using this empty space. This you can see in the obvious basics of perception such as seeing, hearing, smelling, touching or tasting. This reality is not to be taken lightly. The ability to connect with and have awareness levels of other beings, is important to study.

This connecting factor between separate beings is the basis of the mental world. The mental world has been developed as a sort of communication device in which between two people who are conversing you will see a mutual mental world connecting them. This mental world is more than what surrounds them and saturates them. It stretches beyond any known physics of space, size, or time and in fact this mental world that connects your minds today also connects you with the minds of the past. The mental world not only connects you to great creators like Beethoven, Einstein, Buddha, and Jesus, but back to the original Creator as well.

When you truly become a creative part of your world, it's that part of you that will live beyond the life of your body. It may be wisdom, a poem, song, painting, video, or sculpture that wasn't there before. You created it and gave it birth.

The line between mental and physical is easier to measure when you keep them as two separate and different worlds. Exercises in each of these worlds will strengthen your understanding of these separate worlds. Practice closing your eyes, shutting off the physical world and just be a part of your thoughts. Now open your eyes, shut off your thoughts, and just be a part of the world. The more you understand the differences between these two main components in your lives the better you can conceptually connect them.

An easy way to practice separating the two is while eating. This is one of the best times to practice being out of the mental world and into the physical world. Besides evidence that negative thoughts disrupt digestion it's actually fulfilling to just be in the body and taste the flavors. Don't use words to describe the tastes, but rather think with the actual tastes and the sensations. Simply feel the tastes. Experience them. Really get into your animal, physical side while eating. This is a good time to express this animal side anyway.

Many sexual problems arise from being unable to leave the mental world and to just enjoy the physical or animal world. Even those with semi-normal sex lives will have the bliss of orgasm interrupted by the mind coming back to consciousness thus starting all its talking and chattering in the head.

It is possible to stay emerged in ecstasy longer and to avoid the head overpowering your emotions by strengthening the separation of your mental and physical worlds. There are many disciplines that keep life in perspective should you be inspired to study further. You'll find in future chapters that we will delve deeper into fun exercises for the human mind and thus gain a better balance between your physical and mental worlds.

Chapter 4
PHYSICAL & MENTAL

Now that we've differentiated between the physical world and the mental world let's dive even deeper into each separately. When you look closely at yourselves you find that your bodies live in a world of matter, and your heads live in a world of thought. Your understanding of the physical world before you is limited to your perceptions and senses, so let's examine your built-in tools of mental awareness to this physical world.

As you noticed in the last chapter, when two animals, both separate and complete beings, come close enough to each other the emptiness between them magically connects them. The power of visible light bounces off of one animal and into the eyes of the other. This information that passes through the emptiness between them is not to be taken for granted, and makes communication possible.

Smells also travel between you and again information for the brain has traveled from one life-form, through emptiness, to another life-form. Sounds also carry information through the nothingness between the life-forms. Taste will give you information, and so will touching another life-form. You are considered sentient beings because you have awareness and abilities to sense the world outside of your inner selves.

The processes of converting the other person or thing to information that the brain can comprehend still holds that emptiness or unreality between the two.

If a man sees a chair, his mind is working with an image of the chair. Thoughts are not real in the sense that a chair is real (he would get splinters in his brain.) Even if you can't get everything into your heads or composed into thoughts, the reality is still there and does a better job of representing itself. It's like the brain trying to come up with words to describe taste, but it's the sensations of taste that best represent taste.

Reality doesn't need you to figure it out, or name it, in order to run properly or survive. Not only is that not the real world in your head but your eyes are limited in collecting input just as your sense of smell is only one sliver of the total information possible. You all know that dogs can smell more of the spectrum than humans.

You've also heard that most animals have eyes that see in black and white. This seemed weird and hard to imagine, but now scientists tell you that there is no such thing as color in the world of matter. Colors are actually in the different sized wavelengths in light and because all the items out there have different sized surfaces this directly affects the light that bounces off of them into your eyes. The brain then sees the different sized surfaces as different colors in its struggle to break the world into pieces it can comprehend. Brains break the world down to basics like: edges, forms, shading, movement, depth, and even color in order to create a model in the head to think with.

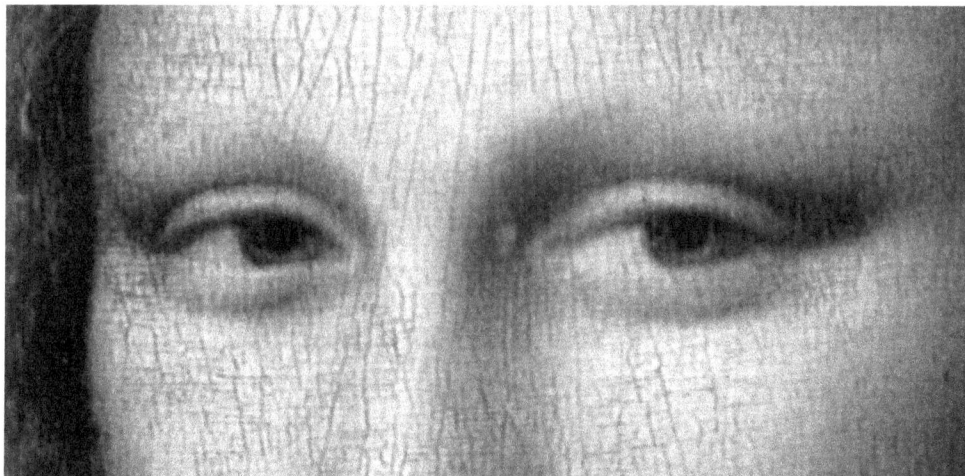

Mona Lisa (Detail)(Oil on canvas) by Leonardo da Vinci (1517)

So right away your perceptions of the world are different than the real world. The human eye is the only animal eye that has a flexible iris making it possible to refocus at different depths. A horse, for example, has eyes that have fixed focus. One side of the eye is focused for seeing things far away while the other side of its eye is focused for things closer. The horse turns its head so that the item of its attention and its distance comes into the right focusing area of its eye.

Most designs of the eyes you'll find in animals are very limited and start with primordial designs that only give information such as lightness or darkness, day or night. More advanced eyes can gather information such as shape and movement. Remember many of these eyes have only one focus such as the 6 inch distance it needs to shoot its tongue out to catch its food. Everything beyond this 6 inches is out of focus and less comprehensible by the mind in question.

This is interesting to humans because their abilities to perceive the world around them is what dictates the perceptions in their minds; which, in other words is the understanding the mind has of the world around itself.

Now once you see that every plant, insect, and animal have different views or mental images that comprise its psyche, you'll realize that your human views may not be as perfect as you once thought. Many of your senses are limited and thus, humans just don't see the whole picture.

Since dogs have higher abilities to smell, you can realize every being around you has different levels of sensing abilities. But with all these many different perceptions and visions of reality, humans must keep the world of reality and the world of your minds as two separate topics; or the world of your minds will gobble you up.

In your mental worlds you can be a king or a queen. In the physical world you are but humble citizens, small pieces of a larger puzzle. Notice when these two worlds are mixed up, you get folks trying to be a God over others. A matured human has an understanding and respect for the true physical world and then secondly their own mental world.

Let's try some mental play. Visualize yourself in a small boat floating on a mirror-like lake. The smell of flowers is all around you. The rocking of the boat. The sounds of nature and water. You've wined and dined yourself and have performed all physical needs required for the day. You've nothing real to do, so you just lay and rest your body. Now you can swim around in your mind, and as you look within all that info pulled in through the senses, arranged to form this mental world of its own, you'll notice you have much power to do what you wish here.

The journey continues beyond your conscious mind and you find deeper intelligences that organize the brain so the consciousness has easy access to all this information. Still deeper you find mind in forms of thought that govern body actions such as breathing, heart beat, and digestion.

Get out the microscope, and mind now is in the little cell that runs around in your body bringing oxygen or fuel to other cells and then heads back for more. Sometimes this little cell gets items from other cells so that it can continue to live. These cells are filled with a nucleus, cytoplasm, and lots of little beings wiggling around inside. You'll find mind, awareness, and thought, both in itself and in each of the little beings wiggling around inside. The stories that all the cells in your body could tell would fill a library.

Physically, you're comprised of the environment that surrounds you. Physically, you're made of the plants, animals, water, minerals, light, air, etc.. The amazing intelligence that designed worms also designed your veins. When you examine your pieces you'll see that you are made with many other, smaller beings.

Your tongue is alive and has its world of thought, and things to think about. It talks to you about things you're eating. In many it dictates what they eat including excessive salt, fat and sugar. Each muscle is a separate snake-like being that although limited, has its place and things to do. It has other beings or muscles around it to live with, think about, coordinate with, and work with.

There are times when fish are brought to the surface and before they can be eaten you'll see their tongue dislodge and crawl from the fish's mouth. What happened is one small animal made its way into the fish's mouth and took out the old tongue. It placed itself into position and acted as a more evolved tongue for the fish. It benefited the fish. This was also beneficial for the smaller animal because it got its share of the food it helped process.

This is a strange fact that you find in nature and what if this helped you to understand all larger life-forms? All the smaller life-forms that move into the bigger cities so that the benefits of combined mutual efforts can benefit the whole as well as each piece.

Let's come back out of your visualization and think about this world around you. Look at all the pieces running around. All those people and other beings. They're easier to pick out than pieces in the body because of the magic space between them. What are humans all a part of? Rather it's a huge being, God or planet is not for your specialized minds to comprehend at the moment, so let's turn back to your roles and the roles of the other beings that make up the bigger picture. The other pieces can be a butterfly or a tree, and you find a new respect for these beings now, because just as you have feelings and thoughts, so does the next creation that flutters by your senses.

Before you will be ready to continue on your path to an advanced, harmonious future you will have to learn this respect for all other beings outside of yourself. Next time you are about to smash a bug, stop and watch it on its little journey. Have fun with the thoughts it must be thinking. The surface that it can't hang onto, kerplop. It falls, composes itself and ventures on.

There are spiders the size of a pencil dot that drop down their own thread and as the breeze blows them around they manage to navigate to the next leaf. There is no avoiding the fact that this speck not only has a mind but is also smart and agile.

The Nest (Oil on Canvas) by Robert-Gavin (1827-1883)

The secret is to empathize with the creature. If you were this bug, happily collecting food for your family, would you think it a kind being that decides to kill you with no mercy? Without even a thought about your feelings? Why were you killed? Not to be eaten, but because the godlike being just didn't like you. A prejudice against your kind, color, or size. Not fair! What kind of godlike being would this human truly be, good or evil?

Imagine a giant being that comes along during your life right when you're having a great time. The giant being looks down on you, lifts its foot to stomp you, but then decides to practice mercy. You get to live. He treats you as he would want to be treated. You've learned a lesson. Now when the little ant drops onto your arm you just laugh and let it continue its life and little journey.

When you can see the fly that bugged you drowning and you rush to save its life, then you will be ready to move on to deeper interactions with the physical world; a world which will save you if you were drowning. Because of the respect and understanding you have developed you will be more responsible with how you use your powers in the physical world.

Now when you examine the mental world you'll find that most of it is intelligence and is used to comprehend the world, co-mingle with the world, and even move the body around in the world. Most of the conscious thoughts that dance in your mind are simply your connections to the world outside yourself. Your creative sides now seem very small compared to all the structured activities and formulas of mind that control your lives in regards to the inner and outer worlds.

As you travel deeper into the aspects of the mental world you find that you can use your mental world to control your body functions. Many humans have learned to stop blood flow, change the heart rate, or to make pain disappear. Sadly, your conscious minds are not as capable or adapted to such thought that run these functions. You bleed for a reason, to flush out unwanted pieces of the thorn, and also the thousands of micro organisms on the surface of the thorn that may be detrimental once inside your system. Your conscious mind should stay out of the way and avoid playing the mental God game on your own body.

Depending on different activities your muscles will need different levels of oxygen, and the blood cells that supply this oxygen are regulated by the heart. The mind and intelligence behind this are well calculated and it works fine, so don't bother trying to take over its job.

If the thorn puncture is producing pain do not stop this process. Your conscious mind may not understand all the activities of the body to fix that hole in your surface. The pain is to the conscious mind only an "ouch," but in reality it is an alert or signal that help is needed in that area.

There are details interwoven in this pain telling certain minds where and what to send in order to fix it. There is quite a lot of information that travels from the wound and the "ouch" that your conscious mind hears is nothing close to the true messages being received by smarter minds beyond the conscious. There are so many little forms of life now that run to that spot to disinfect, clot, scab and rebuild the skin or tissue that you would be baffled if the top mental you, or consciousness, were put in control.

So your top mental world, called consciousness, will instead concentrate on the physical world out there. This is what it has always done so let it do its thing. Now when you set your creative mind to the side of all the other minds you've examined, you'll find that it is as separate a being as all the other minds or thoughts that comprise you. All of your sub-consciousness' that pile up to your consciousness now find on top a whole new mind. An awareness or another whole new sense that taps humans into the larger creative world.

So far you have seen that the power of the mind is used to perceive the world inside and outside yourself. You've seen that your eyes and ears are only extensions of the mind to pick up or sense the outside world. Well there is a lot happening in the world, and as human senses develop, you will absorb more of this magical, physical world into your mental world.

You've seen the many varieties of senses that govern the mental worlds of animals, but it should also be noted that there are more than five senses or ways of gathering information from the world. Some have suggested humans have 22 or more senses, but let's examine the sense of balance. A little structure in your brain holds fluid, that when swished around, tells the brain where it is in relationship to the ground and gravity. Yet another connection, or sense, to the bigger world out there.

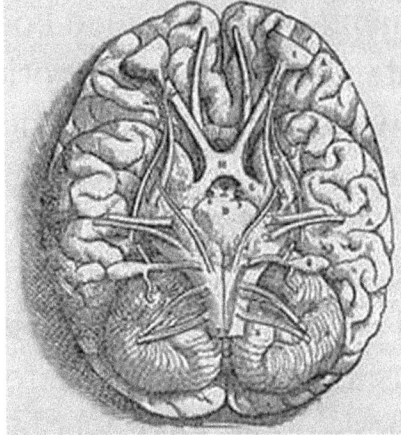

Brain (Sketch) by Andreas Vesalius (1514-1564)

Perhaps it is only a certain flap of brain tissue that happens to vibrate to the song of creativity flying through you? It doesn't matter for the moment. Let this mind mature and develop its creative strengths and it's in this mind that you will spend most of your time. Not in your sub-conscious minds, which handles the thinking inside your body. Not in your conscious mind which collects information outside the body, yet doesn't completely understand the world seen, but in the top mind of creativity that made all the other minds possible.

If you can respect each cell in your body as an

individual that works with all the other cells, then you can realize the you which you have contemplated is simply a cell like any other, but is plopped into the top throne of power. Each of the cells that comprise your bodies have been traveling between plants and animals. These cells have had many different jobs, such as of a cell in a leaf. The leaf is eaten by a beetle and now becomes a part of this new body, for example, a skin cell. When the bird feeds this beetle to its baby, the particular speck is assimilated into the baby bird as perhaps a part of its feather.

Every so often a speck is assigned the position of being a consciousness. As the baby bird was first started in its mother's belly, a speck was assigned this position of power. All the specks are given jobs throughout the body such as being a part of skin or bone but one lucky speck finds itself in the driver's seat.

The odds of sitting in this throne of power just doesn't happen very often and is a blessed thing. Enjoy being in charge now because it may be a thousand years before you, as a cell like any other, get to sit in a throne again, be it a plant or an animal, let alone a human. Don't take this honor for granted. Being a human can be great. Next time you may just be a toad's toenail.

You have better odds of becoming President over a whole country, but wait, you did win the lottery and are

President over your whole body.

The twist is all the inner specks know their places, what to do in the body, and how to work together, but the speck in the outer throne has no set of instructions. This is rather scary and awkward. Don't forget that behind all the other humans, plants and animals are also humble specks which find themselves in similar circumstances and must make their ways in this complicated outer world. Have pity on all those other beings. You are all in the same boat and doing your best to deal with the unknown. It's a lonely predicament. A lonely godliness.

Finding balance with the outer world can be a challenge and sometimes more complicated than the balance found in your inner worlds. Everything has mind, feeling, and thought in common. You each also have the ability to get along with the other beings just as each of the cells inside you get along. Humans can get along with each other. You can find peace. It is a natural process you can learn from nature; the nature created by the intelligence which humans wonder about.

Before you can completely tie your mental and physical worlds together, using creativity, you must examine the higher laws and powers of the Universe. The chapter on the Universe is a very deep place, and you should first lay a foundation of physics, or at least human understanding of physics so far.

Chapter 5
PHYSICS

As preparation to your understanding of the Universe, let's bring to the table everything discovered so far. The Universe may have mostly space, but in the space are many things that humans can't see. Just like the emptiness between you and other beings, there are also magical happenings in the emptiness between the celestial bodies.

Scientists have discovered a whole lot of waves from large to small called the Electromagnetic Spectrum. At one end of the spectrum you'll find the large waves; these are the radio waves. Next come the microwaves and infrared waves. You can sense infrared waves as heat. As the waves get smaller you can then see the waves as visible light. The larger of these waves are red on through the rainbow until the smallest of these waves appear blue. This light you see is about in the middle of all the very large and very small wave sizes out there. Smaller still are the ultraviolet, the x-rays and then the gamma rays, which are smaller than an atom.

Out of all these wave lengths, your senses only pick up a small sliver of this activity in the form of light. You can not see infrared waves, but you can feel them as heat. All those other sized waves just pass through you, or bounce off of you and are not perceived. Or are they? Maybe not by your conscious attentions, but by big and small pieces of yourselves that vibrate when these different sized waves pass through.

Music lesson (Paint on ceramic) Greek Artist (510 BC)

Another discovery has been the principal of sympathetic vibration. If you have two harps and you pluck the A string on the first harp you will notice that the A string on the second harp will vibrate. This is because the physical size of the A string dictates the wave size that it can put out and it's this wave flying around, in that invisible space, that vibrates any strings of the same size.

This is magic. When a piece of matter vibrates it is

moving, and this life action is called animation. The power that gives movement or animation to matter may be invisible to your eyes, but is none the less very real. The matter and forms that move around on this planet operate on a very simple procedure. Sunlight is absorbed by a plant's leaf and converted into sugars and starches. The animals that eat the plants now have energy to move around by firing off their muscles.

The energy that moves their animal muscles can not be absorbed from the invisible space, only the plants can convert the energy flying in from the Sun into energy that can be used to power these other organic life-forms.

Orpheus charming the animals (Oil on canvas) by Francesco Bassano the Younger (1580)

This has been well studied. The plants are the master link in the ecosystem that keeps you alive, and without them all the insects and animals down the line would not survive. So what would make this intelligent human destroy his world? The answer is forthcoming, but we still have to finish your physics lesson to fully comprehend the human dilemma.

There are many studies of physics including the influence that the Sun and Moon have on the tides. Here again is an example of movements by forces flying through the unseen world. The Sun's heat waves, or infrared waves, are what moves the air and the clouds. It also churns the oceans and evaporates moisture into future rain and those amazing lightning storms. You can't see the magic happening behind these events, but the events themselves are real, and have made humans wonder all throughout history.

Further studies have shown that certain waves, or what the experts call radiation, have caused mutations in insects and animals. When the subject is radiated the waves vibrate the subject's structure down to its DNA. The subject then has babies with extra eyes, legs or sometimes no legs. These subjects were called mutants because they were mutated or twisted by radiation to get the new creation, but these always lacked the beauty of the well crafted original model. This destructive wisdom could never measure up to the creative wisdom.

Physics and science have brought humans closer to destroying the fabric of life. The original intent was to understand and learn, but the knowledge of these godlike powers corrupted your young minds, and your civilizations suffered with violence, pain, and unjust use of force and power over each other.

Storming of the Teocalli by Cortez and His Troops by Emanuel Leutze (1848)

What would make mankind do such crazy, destructive stuff? Where does this violence come from?

When you finally admit that humans aren't the biggest deal happening and when the day comes when you question what made a flower, you will realize that there are higher forces. Who created humans? Who created the rabbits or the dinosaurs? Humans have pondered the ultimate questions all throughout history, and are finally ready to meet the Gods (and Devils) responsible for everything so far (including man's violence.) To even peek into the large world that Gods live in; this large world that humans are but only small pieces of.

Chapter 6
THE UNIVERSE

Now that you have learned to respect all forms of life no matter how small, and have admitted that each form of life has levels of mind and awareness, you are ready to move further up the ladder to higher beings. Imagine for a moment, that all the bodies out there from specks and cells, to suns and planets, were endowed with mind and thought. Pick any sun in the universe and look how it boils and moves. Hey, it's moving; technically, it has life. What drives the Sun's matter or body is the basic mind and intelligence that all bodies get. Just like you got and the curious fox got.

Without mind the physical world would just sit there. No movement or action, yet the physical universe out there does not appear to be stupid, and has a lot going on inside it. Here you find the creative formula which when you add matter and soul, thus born is a third new thing; life.

Let's start at the edges and work our way in. The universe is a very large being comprised of a multitude of moving forms inside. Wow, just like you.

This large, alive, being can be examined from

different views to see different sized gears, spirals, and orbits. Scientists in the past searched for similarities such as a solar system to an atomic structure. They found that even the atom took up less than 1% of its space. Between the nucleus, the electrons, and the protons, there was much emptiness. But despite the emptiness between the pieces they stayed joined as one. From what you've seen in the realm of creativity so far, you can now understand what has driven thinkers and philosophers all through history. It's amazing stuff going on.

The Ambassadors (detail)(Oil on oak) by Hans Giovane Holbein(1533)

The time has come to answer the big inquiry of what the universe is, by shifting to what it actually does. The universe accomplishes something after all that work, effort, and activity. Just open your eyes and you will see the light.

Yes, light! That's what is generated by this universe. A sun makes all the other sized waves, but since humans can see light we'll use the light, or visible fire, to symbolize the results of a sun's efforts. This action the fire has of making waves of energy and power can now be appreciated and pinned down. The body of the universe is now seen as comprised of an infinillion number of stars, and these stars are all doing their part.

Remember each star is a sun. Each solar system holds at its core the purpose of its being. Its nucleus and control center. It makes light, and on a very grand scale, depending on the sun being studied. But it was the wise man that looked up, saw the light, and realized that if this giant universal being is making fire and light, then what is a water planet doing here?

What about the influences and laws that govern the solar systems to produce this fire and light? Is perhaps this larger than life, godlike, universal prime direction influencing the humans? This might explain why Sun-God worship has been found in more cultures than any other God. Primitive man used to attribute control of the amazing life around him to the power of the Sun; would it be surprising to find that, although they were primitive and less evolved, they were actually onto something?

Since then, scientists have discovered that the Sun does indeed influence basic movements on Earth such as that of moisture, air and clouds. It also gives movement and power to the life-forms. This is done through heat and radiation, but this same radiation is shown to mutate life. How deeply does the Sun truly affect life on this planet?

If you set aside everything humans have believed up to this point and take a fresh look at how the Sun plays a part, in this stage of life, you may also discover something about yourselves that has haunted your ancestors. What makes humans so evil and destructive?

Earth is in balance between the heat and energy stored up inside, and her cool, watery outside. Inside there is a sea of fire, and the outside shell that floats on the surface is very thin.

Armageddon is a mythical story of humans dying in a sea of fire. What if this was not a myth but an actual possible reality? What if humans kept heating up the planet to the point of raising the molten magma to the surface? Then humans would indeed die in a sea of fire. Not a myth but harsh, painful reality. Not fun.

Just for a moment, picture the molten lava inside of the planet. It is not far below the thin shell of skin that humans live on. The continents (tectonic plates) float and shift above this liquid mass. The hot magma is only down a few miles in fact.

Now picture the bubbling lava rising from a volcano. This is the Sun-like substance which radiates fire and light. If humans, in their own ignorance of what's going on, heat this planet up enough to raise the molten, fiery hell to the surface then all those myths and stories of Armageddon, people engulfed in flames, pain, suffering, and that tragic end will not be some mythical fable but hard reality.

Pandemonium by John Martin (1841)

If humans continue to be influenced by this Fire-God and do not strengthen your earthly, creative powers and alternatives, then humans will be used to make this planet produce fire & light, like the rest of the universe. If humans do take the creative power, and learn to harness it, then you can create anything here, including a heaven or paradise, full of waterfalls, color, life, emotions, creativity and beauty.

Many think that bone is solid stuff but if you hold a human skull cap to your face you will be amazed at how much light passes through. Bone is like semi-opaque plastic. If radiation can move the oceans, mutate animals, and its fingers have such easy access past skulls into human brains, then what is it up to and what does it have in mind? What if it manipulates humans to do things that aren't to their benefit? The Sun has proved to be a higher force on life here, so would it be a surprise to find that the Fire-God/Devil does indeed influence human lives, and humans can be like puppets under its control?

This might explain why the humans were so destructive to their water planet. Even the most intelligent people had their heads in the man-made world and the true physical world was shunned. But as the humans played in their world they would drive around a lot, burn fuel, burn trees and burn each other. They would blow holes in the ozone with flaming rockets, shooting out into space, like a sun sending out a photon; emulating the Sun in a symbolic way.

Step back and you'll see in the real world they were

creating carbons in the air, making the atmosphere more combustible, heating the surface more, and trapping more heat from escaping the atmosphere. Humans then started exploring nuclear capabilities. All this led to one thing: changing the water planet into a fire planet.

Even if it wasn't with a sudden thousand nuclear bombs, or nuclear power plant meltdowns, the slow heating would still eventually lead to the same result.

If humans actually exploded every nuclear bomb they had and consciously made this planet fiery, this power created by man would not even come close to the power created by the Sun. So humans still would not be as big a deal as they thought they were. Yet just a small drop of light in the Universe that makes tons of light. From your two possible futures, water planet, or fire planet, which would you choose?

Another characteristic of mankind is the need to question authority. Where does this come from? Humans play with theories of rebellion and making their own rules and laws. Humans struggle with things that they have to do. Is all this practice for the main rebellion against dying for the universe? You don't want to burn? If humans were still only created animals, life would be a smooth ride off the lemming cliff. But here's the twist in mankind's story. You're able to go against the universal prime direction: make fire & light.

When humans can finally attribute godlike forces and influences to the suns, then it's time to give some validity and respect to the planet Earth. She is also a higher being, a God, and has influence on humans. This planet being has created her own way other than the life of the Sun. Rather than going with the pre-made plan of "make fire" she has used creativity to make herself a unique and amazing planet of water. Is this where humans get their rebel nature? From Mother Earth? Will humans not burn as they're told by the masculine Sun-God?

Humans can do anything, so why not make this tribute to creative power, all the more complex and interesting? Rather than war, she prefers peace, with lots of harmony, color, spectacle, and beauty.

The energy associated with the Sun is shooting outward, yet Earth's energy would be more contemplative and internalizing (moving inward), which most life on the planet appears to be.

But man had this attunement with the Sun's "Go get it" energy and he ran around all day with overzealous, over-energetic, and abrasive actions to normal life on this planet. He used power and manipulation to control and conquer Earth. To attack his own planet with a Fire-God attitude. He manipulated and controlled as a higher force, unaware he was emulating the solar mind of destruction.

Setting the life of a human aside for a moment, let's examine the life and world of the microscopic elements that make up everything.

Some basic activities that matter must endure in life are manipulation, and control by higher forces. The Sun represents a macho energy which smashes atoms (using pressure and heat) for their photons and inner life force without so much as a concern, or mercy, for the structures being smashed and burned. This destructive action, which incorporates forcefulness on matter, is quite the opposite to how Earth acts on matter. Earth uses creativity and harmonies to bring together smaller forms into larger groups. She offers respect to the individual pieces which join to make larger creations. Creations comprised of complex multitudes of cooperation.

She built into the seed the creative abilities and formulas that help it grow with added smaller bits which join and become a creative part of the endeavor. Set the simple plant aside and examine the human body. It is comprised of multitudes of smaller life-forms working together as a creative whole. As you've seen, each blood cell that moves around in the body actually has its little life to live, doing its little actions with all the other little forms, which also play their parts in the whole. This is the magic or power that humans should praise. Power can be used to create, or destroy, to build up, or break down. To harmonize or disharmonize.

The shameful moments in human history such as war, force, cruelty, and violent destruction of life are examples of when the mind of the Sun controlled your motives and actions. The Sun holds down the element, straps it down, and forces its way, ripping photons from it to make light, without empathy. Some men also strapped others down, or used violence and force to tear the person, or other Earth's creation, down to his will. Fire has no mercy and will burn despite how special the being is and despite its emotions and pleas to live.

The martyrdom of Saint Lawrence (Detail)(Oil on canvas) by Titian (1558)

This is the most pervasive evil found to date and it's this evil that humans have to rise above if they are to become civil. True leaders have learned mercy and empathy. It's the "evil" tyrant who cares only about his rule and doesn't respect the life, welfare, and emotions of other creations under his power. If a person is not a creator, they are usually a destroyer.

Humans of the Sun are destructive, uncaring, selfish, and will try to change you if you are different. They use force to bend you to their way. Humans of Earth are constructive, caring, nurturing, and they respect the other creations out there even if they are different. Pyroians will sacrifice every living speck of matter here as fuel to fire a real-life hell. Aquaians will inspire all the elements here to create a harmonic, heavenly paradise, full of water, joy, and creativity. A Pyroian will take pleasure in killing or burning a tree while an Aquaian will take pleasure in planting or watering a tree.

We will explore the relationship between the watery mother Earth and the fiery father Sun in other chapters but for now realize that the Universe has many amazing forms of magic happening all through it. The more humans understand these higher forces, the better chance they will have of adapting to this universal environment and surviving. Surviving, as the specks they truly are, on this bigger stage of the gods.

Chapter 7
GOD

God is a word created to represent the ultimate creator of everything. Man created the word, but you can say that man himself is created by the same Creator that created the word: GOD. In a previous chapter you saw correlation's between creativity and God, so here we will tie together the two concepts into one topic.

Up until this point the word God represented a marker in an equation, holding a place until humans understood what should go there. When humans ask about anything and don't understand, God can be used to explain or fill that blank. All the way back to the beginning of the universe: "Who flipped the switch to turn everything on?" "Who lit the fuse?" If all this was God's idea, then he must be a great and powerful being.

In human attempts to illustrate God's image they have cheated and made him look human, yet even if they could take his picture, this would then only be a symbol of him, and not of the actual power that makes him special.

Now instead of looking outward to other dimensions, let's look into this world, and its realities. The results of

God's work around you can sometimes be awe inspiring, and rather than a picture of the Creator, you can now admire the picture which the Creator made. You can now strive to attain the Creator's mindset and creative intelligence that led to the subject of your wonder in the first place.

Your personal God, that you worship, doesn't have to be a solid image but instead can be the liquid-like thoughts that all creators share. God is responsible for the ideas and equations that give matter meaning, soul, and shape. Even if it turns out to be a solid being that created this life, it would be wise to worship the mind, thoughts, and intelligence that make God so important (just as it's the music you praise created by Beethoven, and not the cells that made up his physical body.)

The human need to attribute the power to a physical form stems from being physical themselves. But even after millions of light years if you reached the surface of the Universe you still would not see the physical form, picture, word, or symbol that you seek. So for the time being, let's turn one's attention from the impossible to the possible and learn to grasp what is right in front of you.

A person can realize, by manipulating smaller life, that he himself is small to bigger forces. As he looks into his own worth and intricate craftsmanship, he is even more dazzled by the awareness that mankind is not the smartest thing around. Neither doctors nor scientists can answer the big questions though they would like to. They can see things that work (like themselves,) but they can't see the forces that made them, or what makes them work.

If humans are to label the main Gods in the arena of life, then the good God is not really the one of light above the clouds as he would have fooled you into believing. The Fire-God, or Devil, also tries to fool humans into going to heaven. He wants you to believe that your home, the Water-God, is the bad God and you should leave. In reality, Earth is where you live, the body that you are a part of, and who you should give your allegiance to. Now instead of looking up to the heavens or the Sun as your supreme master, you now look down at your own world that gave you birth, as the God that really created you, nurtures you, and loves you.

The Sun would have humans sacrifice their lives and bodies to its bidding yet Earth will instead respect you, admire you and encourage you all to grow and live. So now when humans think of a good God that is the grand creator, and a Devil-God that is a grand destroyer, you find things turned upside down. Pointing down at Earth is the good place, and up at the stars is the bad place. Heaven or paradise is here, and hell or fiery destruction is out in the world of the suns.

Amaterasu emerging from Her Cave (Painting) by Shunsai Toshimasa (1887)

The Fall of the Damned (Oil on canvas) by Peter Paul Rubens (1620)

The Fire-God almost had humans bamboozled, but the earthly gift of creativity and its power gave you everything needed to gain control of your minds and souls, thus avoiding the Sun's fiery plan.

Now you start to realize a picture of Earth is a wonderful symbol of a God to worship, better than your images of God so far. Better than all icons created through history. Less fiery than symbols of gods with glowing emanations, halos, sunbeams, or giving off light as the Sun does. You'll find this a lot in past religious art.

As humans mature, their art will be less solar and more earthly. When happy and harmonious people live together in a community of advanced culture, which incorporates the true world of plants, animals, and water, then their basic foundation is as solid as Earth.

Although humans will find themselves adoring her surface, it's her creative God-mind that you will become more connected to. You can worship her body, but now also worship her creative mind, her nurturing soul and inspiration. As you do, your religions and spiritual beliefs will become less superficial, all the deeper, and eventually more refined; further from myth and more down to Earth. Pagan is a derogatory term created by the deceitful God of fire. To worship the God of water, instead of him, brings anger and wrath.

Although the Sun would have humans believe that he

is the true ruler, he is really behind the biggest con job in mankind's history. That sly Devil had humans on the brink of world destruction until he was seen for what he is, as clear as day. Humans saw the light, and their concepts of evil became clear.

Chapter 8
EVIL

Evil is the second half of the duality in religion. There is God, but there is also the Devil. The Devil or Evil has been used to fill in the unknown blank and explain what makes man do things to his and others' detriment. It has been a common belief that there is not only an angel (or conscience that sits on one's shoulder) to help guide a person in decisions, but there is also a little devil (on the other shoulder) that convinces you to make decisions that are regrettable in the long run.

The attributes of the Devil have been fire and brimstone. If you think about the more basic religion of Sun worship you realize that there may indeed be a godlike voice that is, in a strange and deep sense, heard by man. This voice or godlike control hits man on the head and he has looked up to see the godlike Sun hovering above him like a stern parent. We are putting the historic worship of the Sun with the post-modern belief in good and evil, because if hell on Earth did become a reality, this planet would closely resemble the Sun. If Earth indeed heats up too much, the molten core would rise, and after melting the outer shell, would send light out into the Universe.

If religion ceased to be thought of as simply a myth or fantasy, and going to hell, or Armageddon, was realized as reality, then it is quite comprehensible that this planet could indeed be manipulated to resemble the Sun. A Sun which gives off fire, light and other radiation. This all may still seem a fantasy until you take a step back and examine that godlike voice that makes you look up. What is it saying? Why is it repeating itself?

This voice that radiates throughout the universe is the same conversation all the suns sing about. The Sun's motto is intertwined into the waves it emanates just as the voice is intertwined in a sound wave, vision is intertwined in a light wave, and like music is intertwined in a radio wave. What the suns like to chant is very complicated so the easiest translation which humans can understand is "Make fire! Make waves! Make light!"

We have examined in past chapters that this Devil has influenced mankind to manipulate the matter on this planet in such a way as to heat it to glowing lava. This is the same man that can't answer questions like "Why am I here" or "What am I supposed to do" or "Where am I going?" Mankind has been running around without knowing why he is even alive or has been created, thinking he is just doing his job, but really, with all his zealousness and energy he is just doing things that lead to global warming (thus bringing the planet's molten core closer to the surface.) All of these destructive decisions that humans made were attributed to the fiery Devil's influence over their actions during the day.

Rival Sacrifices of Elijah and the Priests of Baal by Lucas Cranach the Younger (1545)

It is interesting to read about the old custom called "sacrifice," and that a sacrifice is burned to appease a God. Lighting life on fire for God was very common. It is also interesting to note that mankind is susceptible to self-sacrifice. This human animal kills itself. Humans kill their parents. Humans kill their children. What makes this so? Is it now possible that man is influenced by higher forces such as a Devil or Fire-God? Yes, it is possible, and a simple look at human entertainment history will show you much killing, hating, sorrow, pain, use of force, lack of mercy, and explosions (with lots of fire engulfing life.)

The concepts of blowing soldiers up in spectacular fireballs or destroying a whole city with just one big bomb are crazy ideas; so what would make intelligent animals do such destructive acts or regrettable sins? A Sun-God, using his power to manipulate you to make a sun or hell on Earth, would make you do such unearthly things. Just look at your quest for more "Fire Power."

The next time you see a barbecue commercial, think about the images they mesmerize you with. The flames grab your attention. Then image after image of flesh, dripping red sauce, browned, charred, and sizzling in fire. Any other animal that eats meat does not fantasize about it looking like that, yet humans, for some reason, use fire (ceremoniously) on most of their food before it's put into their bodies. Charred food was suspected as cancerous and unhealthy, yet humans were so conditioned to put it inside themselves. An unconscious sacrifice to the Fire-God? Packing oneself with combustible and cancer causing carbons? Packing with extra fat for a better burn? Mankind may not understand why he does these things, but the Sun knows exactly what's happening. It's this Fire-God that makes you burn.

There were some children playing when some of this evil got into their heads, and they covered the smallest of them in gasoline. They tried to light the small child on fire, but fortunately the matches also got soaked and would not light. Not all scenarios end so well, and we are left wondering what in the world would make innocent children do something so evil? What got into them? To mindlessly be driven to light another on fire. Where would such an idea come from? A manipulating Fire-God or brimstone Devil would seem to answer this question.

What about that old promise that humans will go to heaven on the big day? How is it possible that humans can beat gravity, leave Earth and ascend into the heavens? It is possible, but forget rocket ships. The fact is, if humans were all burned, their light would shoot away from Earth and into the Universe at the speed of light.

So hooray, humans actually get to heaven, but they find out they are now in the realm of the suns and caught in the basic cycle of forceful manipulation, with the pain of burning. Even going light speed gets boring after a few thousand years. Humans get to travel at the speed of light, but have to *be* light before it will work. It's better to be the self, made of matter, that you already are.

It would be a one in an infinillion chance that a piece of you would end up on a planet like this. A planet like this would be your chance at escaping the cruel realm of the Universe and its suns. A sanctuary. An Eden.

Until this point, mankind just hadn't been such a big

deal. Man was mostly an instinct-driven animal herded by higher forces, and only now has finally moved into understanding himself, his motivations, and his true God. The savior is the God Earth and you should never want to leave her protection. She indeed saves you. The Sun's drive to shoot out into space may have seemed interesting in the past, but after finding that everything out there will kill you, you may decide to become more inwardly driven, like your planet.

Since man has a touch of God's creative power but is unable to grant life, is this why he had used his power to kill and deform? Does this give you a clue to the Sun's mind and maybe you find that the Sun is actually jealous or envious of Earth? When the Sun attempts to be creative he ends up mutating, deforming, or killing. Can't he just admire Earth's creativity?

Many humans, upon seeing someone's creation, will not always be encouraging. Envy drives them to take a negative stance. They become a devil's advocate.

When the Sun does pull something off, is the creation really an offshoot of its negative, destructive, and fiery, core? If the Sun-mind, or intelligence, is behind inventions such as the engine, then it makes sense how an animal could come up with a structure to harness the power of flame. The explosions actually use fire to power pistons which propel the car. This energy was used to drive around in circles, seemingly getting nowhere but back and forth, yet the result from all this was actually heating up the planet. This fire also filled the atmosphere with combustible carbons, like humans did to themselves with carcinogenic food.

Humans usually take things like engines for granted, but when you take a birds eye view of life on the planet you see the humans discovering things like fire, and then gunpowder, and then more discoveries that give him "power" in his life. You have to wonder what makes these crazy animals make these destructive inventions that usually cause death, destruction, fire, and heat. Is the power really yours, or does this destructive power really belong to the mind of the Sun? Are humans just its tools, just as the engine is a tool?

Why in the world do you have people that pour gasoline on someone and burn them alive? That is not thought of by an advanced human, but in the past that was just something that happened. It symbolized a seed core of evil in mankind's nature that couldn't be explained. Now you know, it's the Fire-God/Devil.

It's interesting to examine older explanations, such as astrology, yet we end up again with celestial bodies influencing who you are. Now each fiery constellation has distinctive personalities and times when they dominate those who are born. Each sun may indeed be an individual and unique from the rest, but they still all share the nature to burn. Infinillions of different suns that join the universal chorus with their light, fire and emanations. This prime direction to burn and make light saturates the universe, so it may indeed trickle into your fragile, watery lives.

All through history fire has been used to kill people. Most societies, at one time or another, used burning as a civil punishment. Laws made it normal to not only burn people, but described pouring molten metals into ears and down throats thus burning someone from the inside out. Metal boxes and cages were used to contain people while they roasted to death. Fire, ironically, has been used to burn the evil out of people, and there have been people who have burned themselves. What other explanation of these abnormal behaviors is there?

What would drive these animals to use fire on each other? Be that in a bullet, propelled by a controlled explosion from a cartridge, or be that in a nuclear bomb.

Early attacks involved flinging fire over walls to burn those inside or dropping burning oil on those coming up walls. Bombs were then used to destroy, burn and kill. Things evolved to using the fiery explosions to launch bullets and cannon balls. It is the power of the fiery explosion that makes the bullet or cannon ball travel so fast and with such force. It's fire that also powers rockets to their explosive destinations.

You can find fire power all through human history, yet can humans truly take inventors credit for the physics of fire? Humans didn't invent nuclear fission, but rather were fed the information. Humans didn't create these solar forms of destruction. They've always been here.

When all the people in a community get together and marvel at a fireworks show, is what is driving them simply because it's neat, or is there a deeper Fire-God worship happening on a subconscious level? The fireworks are said to represent bombs bursting in air, but why would these animals be so interested in bombs bursting in air? The other animals run for their lives but humans are like deer in headlights. Maybe the explosions and colorful light are too mesmerizing to look away?

What's happening to human minds when they are mesmerized? If the concepts of mesmerizing someone to get into their heads are true, then the fiery God has more tricks than the zombified humans had realized. Anyone can be mesmerized by fire works, a camp fire, or even a candle flame, to know this is true. To be mesmerized by earthly water, like rain or waves, would be a better choice. If fire can fiddle with the heads of humans, then is this what had driven human animals to create fiery inventions that lead to destruction, death and global warming?

To humans, their actions didn't always make sense and they just did things, but to the mind of the Sun it was simple. The Fire-God is the grand manipulator.

St. Maxim the Blessed by Mazurovskii (1812)

This might explain why whole societies existed on everyone manipulating everyone else. It became normal. In the days of advertising, the idea was to manipulate people into buying something neat for their lives. You have a basic wonder of all the magical creations in life. These things were given dollar values, and used to string humans along using this desire you naturally have for interesting creations. Soon, everywhere a person would turn there was this trickery used to sell them something.

The television was full of ads and sly ways to manipulate people into buying stuff. The newspapers and radios were no different. Billboards filled the skies. Machines called people on the phone to let them know they cared about them, and have special offers for them.

The idea of conning another's mind and whole communities all conning each other is boggling to figure out why, until you see that these are the techniques of the Sun. Family members lying to family members. The Devil that lies and deceives had gotten into human souls. When everyone lies to each other, even to themselves, knowingly and just as a matter of habit, then it's time for some changes. They can't be happy while so disjointed.

How can an advanced people live in peace and harmony if they can't communicate honestly? How can a person live with one's self and the others around him in harmony if he has killed his neighbor? Or slept with his neighbor's wife? Or stolen his neighbor's treasured possessions? These are the sins of the Sun that break the creative spirit, your happy watery lives, and drive you into becoming destructive humans. Unhappy, frustrated, and to the point of accepting a fiery end to the suffering. From an Aquaian to a Pyroian.

Don't accept it. Control your own strings in your daily life, and if you find yourself in a scene getting angry or evil with another, just learn to cool down. Douse the fire. You'll never be happy if you keep fighting. Pyroians make things worse and heat up the battle. How would an Aquaian handle this situation? Pour water on the fire. De-escalate rather than escalate.

Humans need to be on the same team, and you need to use your new creative minds to solve problems with more peaceful outcomes. All the tricks of the Sun to manipulate your minds, lives, and destinies, are seen for what they are, and are considered detrimental to a creative, harmonious collection of people.

You will avoid these sins not because you're told to, but because your heart doesn't really want to destroy your brothers. You really want to live in paradise, to laugh, to admire friends, and to be admired. To treat others as you want to be treated. Not because you're forced to get along, but because you want to get along.

Advanced humans that have learned to redirect the Sun's energy and not let it make them destructive, will learn what real freedom is. Freedom from unfair rule and from tyrannical control; freed from being manipulated, but now with the responsibility of being in control of yourself and governing your own life from within. Just like the cells that live in harmony in your body, you also have this earthly desire to be a part of the bigger group.

What you want from another can not be burned from their bodies. Peace does not come from using fire power.

You've made a full circle back to the beginning and you find one of the first fables put into the mind of man by the Sun. Humans all have read that man discovered fire, and this marked a crucial turning point in his history. We can now see that it was really fire that found man, and said, "Wow, interesting, I can use this." Into the mind of man it went; but like a cosmic game of rock/paper/scissors, water beats fire. Your new watery religions and creative goals are more powerful than the destructive fire power.

The energy expelled by the Sun then just becomes energy used for your own means, just as the plants use this simple wisdom. Its attempts to manipulate you are redirected and refocused using a jungle canopy of trees and leaves above. Capture those waves before they enter your brains. Reuse that bad power for good. The dispersed light left over is further restructured by your watery prisms and lenses of creative thought.

You can't kill this radioactive devil, but you can intelligently understand his power and put this power under your own control, just as the plants do. Use it for its raw energy. Use it for vision or for warmth.

When you use this power alongside the power of creativity, you are officially in the realm of the Creator, Earth; with the power of life in your hands. This is much more rewarding than the old-fashioned power of death in your hands.

Learn to be humble. Your creations are fun and amazing, but you are still just animals playing with creative, godlike powers. Humans are still learning and still can't make a true life-form; to give something life, as Earth gave you. Humans only create symbols to represent this life creating power.

It's okay if your creations don't have independent souls or can't reproduce. That is your creator's job, Earth, and this job is nothing close to what you can handle or take personal credit for (just as your conscious mind doesn't try to take the jobs away from your bodily minds.) Crossing these boundaries can lead to complex troubles.

Both mankind and the Sun can take credit for the creation of the car, but the car is still only a mechanical copy of the truer organic life. It is an interesting creation, but nothing close to the complexities or the mechanics of a small rabbit. The automobile represents an active and live being, but only in the most sophomoric of ways.

Created to resemble processes known in life, it has fluids, veins, and movements. It also has input and output. In goes fuel, and out goes work. It does something, and because of these accomplishments, has a meaning and purpose in life.

The Sun's creations, although interesting and neat, don't come close to Earth's magical seed that can grow into a mighty tree. Note that water is a trees friend and fire is its enemy.

Jupiter giving fire to Vesuvius (Ceiling Fresco) by Francois Joseph Heim (1841)

Which is more valuable? The earthly gift of watery construction or the solar gift of fiery destruction?

Man's understanding is miles away from the complexities of making even a one celled protoplast. A protoplast which has the ability to convert the Sun's energy to organic forms that sustain life (such as sugars, starches, and ozone.) Humans, and other animals, cannot directly convert the Sun's energy to organic nitrogen compounds, but those green plants do have this intelligence.

To do this, the leaf takes a carbon molecule from the air, makes the photosynthesis conversion, and the exhaust from this action is a molecule of oxygen. The engine is similar, but actually reverses the process. In goes oxygen and out goes carbon (which can be burned if conditions are right in the atmosphere.) Most of the world works because of this simple conversion of a photon form of energy or fire into an earthly, organic energy harnessed into matter, and then used to power the machinery of the animals. Carbohydrates are like charged batteries that can hold the Sun's energy for later.

In nature the plants are then eaten by herbivores. The herbivore animals and insects use the energy in the plants as fuel to fire off muscles and move around. There are actual small explosions, inside the muscles, that supply the power and energy that moves the limb. This gives them the power to move and animate.

An herbivore can eat a plant to get protein for making its muscles but the carnivore can't. The carnivore must eat the herbivore to get protein for its own muscles. They both eat carbohydrates to power those muscles.

Humans interestingly are in between. Humans can directly use protein from plants and/or animals, making them omnivores; but that's for proteins that make muscles. For energy and carbohydrates to power the muscles, humans must fill themselves with plants constantly or die. Therefore, to get both proteins and carbohydrates from plants makes sense.

Many people that have become vegetarians did so because they developed an empathy for the little animals after realizing they have feelings, emotions, and souls also. When humans live with animals, they are constantly amazed at this creative and intelligent world.

In happy little villages you'll find humans going about their day surrounded by nature and animals. Elephants help some humans carry heavy things while the mischievous monkeys steal a melon from a tradesman (who shouts and waves his arms, but then chuckles to himself.)

Talk about life. Thick like a stew. Happy people, animals, and plants. The cities of the past had their problems with people going crazy. So now the cities of the future incorporate the real, physical world into their man-made worlds. Cities filled with plants, animals, and waterfalls give the people a more balanced world and mindset; an Aquaian mindset.

Cities of the past had cut down all their trees thus exposing themselves more to the Sun. The asphalt got too hot to walk on. This not only added to global warming, but gave better access to the brains of those

Sun Soldiers/Pyroians running around all day. Cities of the future are covered in a canopy of leaves which catch the Sun's rays before they hit the human heads, and remember these leaves can then convert the Sun's power into raw, earthly energy to be used down below.

The ground is full of microscopic life. It's also been shown that once the canopy of leaves above are cut down and the Sun is allowed to hit the ground, that the Sun's rays actually kill the microscopic life-forms. The ultra-violet light ionizes these little life-forms by ripping out their electrons and leaving electrically unbalanced atoms. Many of the very small, microscopic life in a forest lives because the green leaves above catch the light before it hits them. These leaves then convert the light into positive, organic sugars, which filter down to this life on the forest floor and makes the chain of life possible.

It's that simple. As an educated human, the thoughts now of wiping out forests to raise hamburgers is silly and downright dangerous to a healthy planet.

Once humans have learned to avoid the evil influences of the Sun and the human personal powers of mind rise above that of the Sun, then you will eventually see its power as simple fuel for your own endeavors. The images of this flaming Devil-God are useful for escaping his influences, but he can not be killed or destroyed. To kill a killer, or evildoer, doesn't equal peace, it just makes you now the most destructive force; worse than the destructive force you conquered.

Countries have gotten tired of corrupt larger countries, and have eventually risen in power to overtake them, and each of what started out the mistreated became the mistreater. The solar disease of corruption is contagious. Fighting fire with fire is yet another mischievous misdirection by the deceitful Sun-God.

Deep in the past there were civilizations that each rose in power and the power corrupted them. Their misuse of power caused the next to eventually overtake them. But because the next had risen in power above the power that had hold over them, the corruption again turned the oppressed into the oppressors.

Because powerful countries had used power to oppress, bully, and manipulate other countries, they risked falling into the same old cycle found throughout history. A cycle that made humans meaner and meaner.

Is it possible for your country to treat other countries with respect just as a wise person treats another person? Instead of being domineering and tyrannical could countries harmonize as teammates in a bigger game?

Since a country is really a cluster of people, then it's the people that have to fix their perversion with power. Each human has only to examine his own evil nature to control or overpower another and change this to thoughts of how he would like to be treated. If you don't want someone to govern your life, then don't try to govern their life. If you try to overpower them then you fall into the same old cycle that civilizations have always fallen into. They will try to overpower you. To fight evil with more evil you will not win, but lose even more.

Let's examine this on a personal level. If a person is constantly overpowered, as they develop, they will compensate by learning to fight back with more power. A person that develops in a nurturing environment will not become a tyrant but instead becomes a nurturing person.

When humans talked of gaining power, and getting their way over weaker powers, is it humans that are winning, or does this power really belong to evil, and it's evil that really wins in the bigger picture? The Sun-God makes humans war but even in the final nuclear war there would be no true winners other than the Fire-God.

So to rid your psyches and your societies of evil, you will have to limit your exposure to the Sun and then keep aware of how you intermingle with the world around yourself. Treat the other beings just like you would want to be treated. If you do not like over authoritative people trying to control your life or mind, then you must not treat others that way. Instead just see the others' way as interesting, and as just another choice or alternative. Nothing says that you must adopt it. The other person may even have some good ideas.

If you catch yourself trying to force your way on another being, just stop and take a deep breath.

Scipio Africanus Freeing Massiva by Giovanni Battista Tiepolo (1719-1721)

Let your tyrannical side melt away and bring in your side that practices acceptance. The more you just accept others for their differences the happier you'll be. Those that are driven by the Sun's Pyroian mindset try with all their might to change those around them, but will never be happy, and will be constantly frustrated.

Experts have always said this. Troubles between married couples usually come from one trying to change the other. But if the other doesn't change and stays different the first will grow angry and frustrated. Advice to these couples is usually to give up trying to change the other, and the frustration will melt away. Learn to accept the other for who they are, and you also are accepted for who you happen to be. It's now a fact, someone that always tries to dictate his ways to others, or is overly headstrong and bullheaded, will never be happy.

No one likes to be dominated and what you really need for happiness are but a few basics: acceptance, encouragement, and praise. When you *accept* others and are accepted, there will be no strife. People get into a lot of trouble trying to be accepted.

In a balanced society you will all accept each other no matter how different. In fact, because you represent the common belief in creativity, the more different you are, the more accepted you are.

Now let's move on to the concept of encouragement. Whatever creative project you are working on, be it a song you are making, or a sculpture, there also needs to be *encouragement* from those around you. It is so easy to over criticize the artist, and after a certain amount of negativity the artist will lose his drive, and the creation will suffer. Instead be positive to those creating something. Be on their side and *encourage* them. When humans stop opposing each other and are all instead on the same team, then your creations will soar.

Finally, learn to honestly *praise* the accomplishments of others. Sometimes humans let their admiration turn to envy, and this evil can very much hurt the artist, and future endeavors including your own. One of the great elations in life is when you are praised by your fellow people. This actually releases endorphins into your blood, and makes your whole body feel good. It makes you happier with yourself, and in better balance internally, so that then your future creations can continue to mature. But these things which are needed to keep your mental balance, must also be given to others so they can have mental balance as well.

As you look into your soul you will find that you can use your powers for good or bad, to encourage or discourage. If you let the Sun-mind spit insults out of your mouth to another, you have now used power to hurt someone. If you instead use your earthly power to make someone happy, you will also find an internal happiness inside yourself, and a stronger, more mature power. If you had the choice of making someone hurt or happy, which would you choose? How about turned around, would you want someone to use their power to hurt you, or help you? The more tuned in you are with how you want to be treated by others, the better you will treat those same others.

Once humans as individuals have toned down their evil sides, they will find that their societies will reflect these changes. Countries will now be ashamed to be caught using fire power, or Pyroian dominance over other countries. An Aquaian country will appreciate different countries, and instead of trying to change them, will offer acceptance, encouragement, and praise.

We've seen all through history civilizations rise and fall. Even what once appeared as unconquerable, always eventually loses top power and is conquered. With this in mind, it might be wise for the top country as a whole, to take advantage of your power while you still have it, and use it in more responsible ways.

While you still have the power you can change the games that the world plays towards more productive and intelligent directions. You can show how you would want to be treated if and when the tables are turned. Rather than dominate, use power to inspire. With the world's eyes watching you could set examples of harmony and creativity. Show that the old problems of manipulation and violence can be overcome, and the rewards are great.

The further away humans get from the sins that pushed them apart and caused imbalances, the closer they will grow. The deeper their individual spiritualities will develop. When humans have similar spiritualities, you find that, there in between, in that mental world that connects you all, there will develop a common religion which will tie you all even closer together.

Chapter 9
RELIGION

Separating the difference between religion and spirituality, you realize that it's your spirituality that represents your internal beliefs and laws that you live by. You learn spirituality from experience. It's how you internalize and see the amazing world around you. A religion on the other hand, is a belief system shared in common with many others. You learn the words that describe others' experiences. When many people have the same spirituality, only then it is a true religion.

So what happens when you learn a religion instead of your own spirituality? You then take the attitudes and beliefs of others and take them for yourself without actually feeling them in the first place. This can be frustrating because a person will end up with just a bunch of words that are in the head, and no true spirituality in the heart. Humans have seen a lot of this in their troubled past.

Just for fun, let's examine how in many people's upbringing they learned to laugh at the idea of God and then commenced to live evil lives. Back when the kids were brought up believing in Santa Claus. He comes to humans, from above, through the FIRE place. This mystical character with godlike, magical powers knows when you've been good or not. He also distributes the many items and treasures as gifts to your lives and so forth. But isn't this very similar to the stories of God that kids are told? He also is a mystical character with magical powers. He also knows if you've been bad or good. He also is responsible for what you get in life.

Santa Claus by Thomas Nast (1872)

But from these two mystical characters you find out that the first was just a lie. You were deceived into believing in him. It required blind faith because you never got to actually see him. When you were young and developing, you all gave in, and for many years actually believed in Santa Claus until the day came when you found out the truth.

The whole world was lying and there wasn't really a Santa Claus. It was really a Dad, or other human, that played the part and left the gifts. It was a mortal that gave the magical items you got in this world. Not only was Santa all a grand lie, but each child gets to the age when he must now lie to his younger brothers and sisters. He is forced to make them believe that Santa is real, to now pass the lie. To tell the truth would be a sin. Also, note all the Christmas trees that are killed in this ritual.

After all this, the young person reflects on the second mystical character he was told to believe in; God. Is he really going to blindly believe in this similar character? Probably and usually not. There are always doubts. All kids in ponderous moments ask each other if they believe in God. Many times they come up with logical reasons why they don't believe in this character that sees all. They then ran around getting into mischief and could be quite the little devils sometimes.

This is part of a game which humans didn't realize they were in. The fiery God of deception boosted their egos and had the humans thinking they were in charge, that they were the most powerful gods on the planet.

When everything around you is man-made, as you

will find in a city, then man becomes the powerful God that's made everything. Before you know it the questions of higher forces are never even noticed. God was supposed to be that higher intelligence behind the magic in the world of nature, but now man is praising himself as the biggest deal around. They cut down nature and built a man-made environment. Kids started believing that it's really a man in the God costume. Man is the God behind the man-made world everywhere they look. They don't see trees and animals, but cement and buildings.

Older texts may tell folks not to commit sins but the human tests his power and finds that he can do anything he wants to do. It doesn't seem to hurt when he sins so he sins more and more. By then, beliefs in both Santa Claus and God are laughed at. He now plays Santa to his kids. He is the God of the world he sees. He doesn't have to be good or bad. But even though humans play gods and do whatever they want, you'll notice that they aren't really happy or balanced. They fight, steal, kill, and degrade each other, and instead of being a bunch of gods they actually are a bunch of devils.

So how do humans avoid this road to unhappiness? First you must treat your children with respect and honesty. Do not fool them with stories of Santa Claus, Easter Bunnies and mythical gods, but instead tell them stories more down to Earth that will benefit their future lives. There are many communities that speak to children normally, and as if they were adults. No baby talk or deceitful stories. These children grow up more balanced adults and in turn raise more balanced children.

Instead of forcing a religion down a child's throat, you should encourage them to find the keys of happiness in their own hearts. To explore their own spirits. While playing together they will learn what they do that causes happiness, and what causes unhappiness. Even with puppies you'll see in their play that one may bite too hard, the other cries out loud, the first then learns not to bite so hard, and how to play fair.

Suspense by Charles Burton Barber (1894)

You can offer guidance, but only a skeletal structure. They will fill in the meat. The stories you will tell your children in the future are of happy humans that get along, and you will never fill their heads with things that they shouldn't do.

Many folks have learned in psychology classes that if you tell a child to stay out of the cookie jar, that this itself will draw the child's attention to the cookie jar. Humans can do almost anything, and when your minds hear something to not do, the *not* disappears from the sentence, and it becomes something you can actually do.

If you tell someone over and over "do *not* steal" they will be haunted by "do --- steal." This is basic psychology and yet it is not seen in most religions or laws of the past. So let's practice turning to positive tools of thought. Instead of "Thou shall not kill", change this to "Thou shall help life." Now the mind is not frustrated by lots of stuff *not* to do, but instead by what *to* do (which is what it all comes down to.)

But why should humans have to do anything? You can do anything you want, so why should you limit yourself? The answers are simple. To have a happier, more balanced life. To get along with others. To keep yourself safe from retaliation. To have a righteous and healthy life. Avoiding sins, or following commandments, were really only attempts to avoid living with regret, pain, mental imbalance, and unhappy lives.

Sure, you have the power to kill your neighbor, but

this act will haunt a person's soul for the rest of his life. This has been the main problem with many soldiers that have returned from war. When they joined they were just young adults with lots of energy, and a need to please. Their future seemed to be an exciting drama in life to experience, much like what they had seen in movies or television. But in an instant, a trigger is pulled, and he has destroyed another life, or his partner beside him dies while holding his own intestines. The reality of death and destruction then overwhelms his soul, and obtaining happiness will be very difficult from that point on.

A happy, well-balanced human feels good about himself and would be tormented by his own regrets, conscience, and sense of imbalance if he had stolen from a friend; so he doesn't steal. Not because it's a law, but because it will break his happiness, balance, and godlike connection with the world he's a part of. It's that easy.

Religions and laws want people to act good and to not sin. What if the angle this is dealt with, is changed? From cramming your head with bad things not to do, to instead, giving you good things to do? In other words, if rather page after page of what is bad, there was page after page of what is good? What if, instead of others having to control or force you to live correctly, you do it because you want to? To have the wisdom inside yourselves to shape how you interact with the world. A wisdom coming from inside of you rather than from outside of you. When humans rewrite simple suggestions to avoid sins, you won't find the words "Don't be Greedy." The words will read "Be Generous and Share." "Rejoice" is much better than "Don't wallow in sorrow."

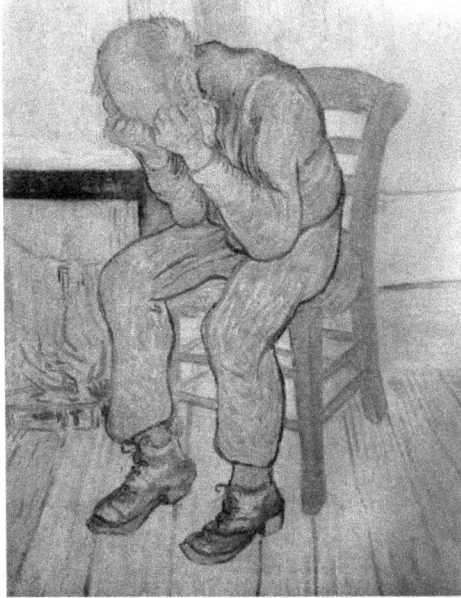

Old Man in Sorrow (Oil on canvas) by Vincent van Gogh (1890)

Now that's a righteous life. When each person has learned the right from the wrong, Earth's influences from the Sun's influences, the good from the bad, they can then govern themselves. You will then find that the questions of violence, destruction, and sins of the past can be easily answered and solved. Once this wisdom is in each of you, all of you can join to create more advanced communities, and better harmonized societies.

Chapter 10
SOCIETY

Society is a group of people that live together as a part of a bigger group or working system. Even a family household is a society in that the whole can be seen as a series of smaller pieces. The husband builds the table, the wife cooks the food, the son waters the garden, the daughter collects the eggs and milks the goat.

Whatever parts they play, the combination of these constitute a whole. On a bigger scope, the town where they live can be seen as a whole, and also is made up of the smaller pieces such as the farmer, baker, and candlestick maker.

A wider scope shows the country as a whole summed by parts (the towns, cities and states) and it's this that is normally termed society.

Your body is a society of smaller life-forms, townships, and cities that work together to create your larger form. The more you realize this, the more you will be amazed at the complexities at work here. If you compare your body to a country, you end up with a similar description of the world. Lots of smaller pieces all working together, in groups, as a larger whole.

La Mi-Careme (Oil on canvas) by Fritz Zuber Buhler (1822-1896)

A happy whole, comprised of happy pieces. It's entertaining to imagine when a pool of water is inhabited by a community of life-forms that they find a balance so that survival for them all is assured. As the pool becomes thick with life, you notice it becomes a larger being comprised of intertwining plant life and tiny animals. The pond is alive and a being in itself.

The pool-being and society inhabitants move around each other just as in the human system. The plant life thickens, wraps around each other, and comprises the solid circuits, veins, and pathways that tiny animal life-forms live and travel in. The plants supply things that the animals need, and in return the animals supply things that the plants need, and so forth.

Even inside the plants themselves you can see smaller animal-type forms that move around. In fact, many different types, all working, exchanging, and nourishing each other. Lots of little pieces running around, back and forth. The same is inside the human body. The same is inside human societies. There is a matrix of life in everything you may decide to study.

As human communities fuse together to become one, who's to say the pool or body of water doesn't also eventually start moving around and begin the cycle again by joining with other bodies of water? Similarly, we are getting closer to the core of future human societies; advanced societies where humans harmonize and create together.

Painting breathes life into sculpture (version 2) by Jean_Leon_Gerome (1893)

So what happens when one of the pieces in a puzzle is uncooperative? Instead of working in harmony with the other pieces in a state of humbleness and devoted to the bigger being, you find a cell that tries to take over? Take over as a selfish, egotistic, separate self with Fire-God attitudes? In a human body, this cell would be called a cancer. This cancer uses its power to pull other cells to its side; to follow its blueprint rather than the hosts, and to manipulate other cells to disharmonize with the host.

As this new being develops and grows you find no regard for its host, and without mercy or respect the host is eventually killed. This tiny speck operates from the Sun-mind of destruction, and uses its power to take over the host's humble mind of creation. This same tiny speck is sometimes the carcinogenic burnt remains of something eaten. Something burned with fire. Something a destructive thought said to put inside the self.

When you examine Pyroians, the humans that operate from the Sun-mind, you find that when you pull back to see the bigger picture that these humans are also just specks of cancer on the skin of Earth. They also are destructive to the bigger whole, and they also pull other humans to their side, thus growing stronger, and taking over more and more others. The people are like the cells that are told to reject their harmonious blueprint. The reward that the cancer gets is the same death that it brought to its host. After all that work, it is just as sacrificed to the Fire-God as the being it was driven to destroy. It was deceived and blinded to the greater truth just as the Sun will blind you from physically seeing.

If the cancer knew about the destructive forces that drove it, and the death that was coming, do you think it would continue? Would it then have more of a reason to let go of the evil influences, and embrace the laws of harmony and the life that it tried to destroy? Because of survival and intelligence, it would probably choose life.

What would you decide? If you choose to give up your evil side, and to strengthen your harmonious side, then you would be a perfect piece in an evolved society. Just like the perfect cell in a body, you would give nourishment to the body that you comprise, and would never think of destroying the body which gives you what you need to live in return.

In a corrupt system you can argue with your rebel nature, but what if you were in a healthy system which you agreed with, didn't have to fight, and even made you happy?

The concept of a civilization is that its members are civil. Civil means cooperative, respectful, and with consideration of others. Were your past cities really civil? Were the individual pieces considerate to each other? When your city members find this earthly, mental state, you will be closer to the mental state that makes the body of an animal possible.

A good example to study is the body of the Portuguese man-o-war. It may look like a jellyfish but it's really a colony of many microorganisms that organize and come together to create the larger being. Scientists don't consider it an official animal but instead call it a "siphonophore." The many small life-forms that comprise it are called "zooids" and truly need each other to survive. This is a good example of Earth's creative power, potential, and growth through cooperation.

Most cells or organisms would much prefer to live in a body that is strong with harmony, and not filled with cancers. An innocent human that moves to a city filled with Fire-God manipulated Pyroians realize they are in a dangerous, cancerous place. Humans prefer cities of the future like happy cells prefer a happy body. Survival, safety and harmony are more assured in an Aquaian city.

So now the day has come when you can join other earthly groups of people, and not fear the destruction and sins of the past. Societies that practice harmony and fulfilling life. Now that you find yourself making love instead of war how do humans civilly handle sex? In the past, human sexual drives were considered sins. Is sex really a sin or can humans incorporate sex into future, advanced societies without becoming perverse?

Chapter 11
SEX

Sex is the marvelous process that is involved between two bodies in order to create that fresh new, third body. It's how animals make babies. We've seen that sex is more than sensations of feeling good. It's incentive to physically procreate. Many have not understood what is behind this powerful drive, and yet it controlled much of their lives and subconscious directions.

The Sweetheart (Oil on panel) Hugo Kauffmann (1890)

We have noted that it's a creative spirit that brings together individual beings to result in new things, and that this is done with the cooperation of the original pieces. When two humans take the positions of the cooperative separate pieces, and come together in a mutual bonding of bodies, minds, and hearts, then usually the creative power will flow through them in such powerful ways as to surpass words. They become one, an Androgen. Two halves together to make one whole human. The physical and mental occurrences that surround sex and orgasm are mystical, amazing, and wondrous, yet modern societies raise people to shun, laugh at, or abuse this topic.

Instead imagine an advanced society where its people understand their bodies, and their bodies in relation to the other bodies.

The media of the past had taken advantage of human needs for sex, their lack of education on this topic and the time has come for some basic understanding of this magical process. A well-balanced person is connected with all the physical functions and will not attempt to avoid such knowledge. You can roll on the ground giggling forever, but that doesn't change the serious fact that you eat, excrete, breathe, flatulate, burp, perspire, menstruate, lactate, ejaculate, ovulate, and have sex. To mentally look away from such realities removes you further from reality, and from living comfortably within your physical and mental worlds.

Mature people don't cuss because they don't attach bodily functions to frustrating moments. Cussing doesn't do any good, yet strengthens the connection between aggravation and the basics of one's life. The words are used to express anger and frustration yet the words themselves mean normal things like going to the bathroom and sex. The true, deep frustration comes from societies making reality a taboo.

Knowledge of reality must be encouraged so that it becomes second nature. No more cute stories of storks or other blatant, frustrating lies. Sex is real no matter how hard old societies tried to make it taboo.

Go ahead and admit that sex is pleasurable. It really feels good. But this is your conscious mind saying "wow" when there is really much more going on. Like the "yum" from taste is a secondary sensation when really you are filling your body with food. The amazing creator of your body tantalizes you to reproduce by also using simple pleasures and rewards. Yes, there is so much more than that "wow."

If an inquisitive child wants to know about sex or what the word means, keep in mind they won't understand the physical part until their bodies mature so you can keep your answer down to ways in which couples live together as mates. You can keep it simple and tell your child that, "As people grow up, they will fall in love, live together happily as husband and wife, and have children." They will figure out the physical details later when they are ready.

Adults raised in a society based on media exploitation make sexual understanding amazingly difficult. The effort required would be so much more than if instilled at the proper young age, so start fresh with your children. Give them the upbringing you should have gotten.

The old media had latched onto the courtship stages and perpetuated them throughout life even when a suitable mate had been obtained. The old media encouraged a train of thought for finding a mate, and failed to supersede this with knowledge about happy adult family life after the mate had been found. Flirting became second nature, and almost always interfered with the actions following the attraction, such as living together, and raising healthy children. Television showed families being selfish, rude, degrading, and lying to each other, followed by canned laughter to make it fun.

In an advanced society where people respect and admire others that are different and creative, you'll find relationships based on truth rather than superficiality. If a couple is attracted to each other for who they are, and not just how they appear on the surface, then you get true chemistry. Anyone can be attracted to someone's outer shell, but it's the deeper connections that make a long-term relationship. The love and sex between them results in a baby, thus completing the circle of life.

Daphe and Chloe (Oil on canvas) by Louis Hersent (1777-1860)

In physics, when two waves come into sync they intensify. Two waves in the ocean that combine become twice as high. Two waves of sound that come into sync become twice as loud.

When two humans are making love their hearts actually start beating at the same rhythm. Their breathing also comes into sync. There are a whole series of things that come into sync, and each is amplified beyond what each could do individually. The "wow" that the couple feels is intense because of all the syncing going on and the results of the intensified rhythms; just like the two sound waves that become louder only when combined.

When human bodies get to a point where everything is in sync, the magic of creation overwhelms them. It's a similar bliss that the elements feel when they become one. It's a treat from Earth for willingly giving yourself to the larger creative endeavor. Giving in to the Sun leads to pain, but giving in to Earth leads to pleasure. It feels good.

It's interesting to note that humans come in both male and female models. The deeper you explore the masculine aspects of the Sun and the feminine aspects of Earth, you notice women have more of an emotional side, and men have more of a cerebral side. Through history women have created by giving birth, and men destroyed by killing. Women have been nurturing and loving, while men have been tormentors and haters.

Somehow women were more influenced by the creative Earth, and men were more influenced by the destructive Sun. When you examine a couple you quickly see the difference between the male and female. The female is very beautiful and is crafted with a delicate touch. The male is similar, but with a touch of the radiation that mutates the beauty out of life.

Take a moment to study the faces of men and women. You can see the mutant effects of radiation on men's faces. Fire's been burning at men's souls for thousands of years. It very well may be that men vibrate a bit more to the Sun's wavelengths, and women more to Earth's vibrations. It's men that need the most re-tuning.

For years women have wished men would be more in touch with their emotional sides, but society would persecute them if they didn't conform; now it's allowed. It's healthy to strengthen the watery sides of being a man and makes it easier to get along with each other than using your fiery natures. A man can still take charge, but now with things like creative projects.

In the balanced cities of the future, men will not be expected to be the destructive soldiers of the past, but the creators of the future. Much more refined and less barbaric. As men and women find a balance in themselves and their society, they can then mate in natural, healthy ways.

Rather than unwritten laws of courtship, you'll find in a balanced city that the mating dance is made easy. The young or single can wear a symbol or special ornamentation that represents their single status. Each can see the others that are not yet coupled. Then one may ask another to spend some time together. They can learn about each other, and see how it feels to be with the other. The steps can be made easy for those young and single souls that only want love in their lives.

Once a mate is found, the symbol or special ornamentation can be removed to indicate you are no longer single.

Just as you don't need to explain certain details to curious children, the same logic will be used here pertaining to the actual act of sex. It's more than a penis, a vagina, a sperm and an egg; there is love. Once you have matured physically, emotionally and mentally, you will then be ready for marriage and kids (along with the fun of figuring out how.) A lot can be written on the topic of sex, but it's better to experience it first hand; to develop your own personal, deep understanding of this powerful creative force. Just like love it's more bonding, as a personal journey that is, experienced together.

When your lives are in balance and your sex lives fulfilled, you'll start to see everything around you differently. Beside the people, animals, plants, and other earth-made things, you have your man-made things. All these earth-made and man-made things used to be valued in terms of dollar/number worths. This archaic economic formula created imbalance, separated people from reality and made advanced, harmonic life difficult.

Chapter 12
MONEY

Money, as most people didn't realize, was not a real thing and was comprised only in the head. It was based on a value system that attempted to categorize everything real into a mental data sheet. It had been the way to see something and its worth on the totem pole with everything else. People thought that all they really wanted was a lot of money. What they really wanted were the things that the money would buy; the food, shelter, clothes, toys, tantalizing pieces of the world, etc..

To understand this, with simple mind play imagine that you are trapped alone on an island, and you find a treasure chest with five million dollars inside. After an exclamation and maybe rolling around in it, you'll slow down to a point where you just stare at it. You can't eat it. You can't make clothes much less build a home with it. Money can do nothing for you other than its mental worth in a system of people trading for needed things. Take out your money. Look at it for a while. After a few moments it begins to look exactly like what it is, paper. On the island, you would trade it all for another person.

Money is only worth what is believed; like what

makes Santa Claus real is people believing he's real. As you mature you'll find it is not money that's real but the pieces of reality you can buy, that's real. Pieces of the mutual world aren't yours, or a part of your personal world, until you buy them. Who says and by what right?

The Calling of Saint Matthew (Oil on canvas) by Caravaggio (1599-1600)

This is not the true natural value system that Earth uses. Soon in the new creative societies money will not be used or even remembered. Each creation, big or small, will not be seen filtered through a number worth, but through a visual sense of just what it is. A corkscrew is not equal to one dollar but is equal only to the corkscrew that it is. Its usefulness also can't be described by a number.

Limiting the worth of every item to a number is as bad as limiting the flavor of a cherry to the word cherry. There are deeper ways, other than numbers, to sense and find values in pieces of the world. Art can be the proving factor. Just look at 1,000 different paintings (with the same price tag) and you can see that each one is different, yet equal to and worth exactly itself. Therefore, everything is priceless from the flower, to the world, to the universe. You are worth exactly...you.

Needs such as food, water, clothes, and shelters are automatically met in an advanced society rather they use money or not. Trading avocados for oranges was fine for a time, but if the community has a hundred people, then the avocado man simply makes sure there is enough for everyone. That, in a sense, is his job. Get a hundred avocados to the big kitchen.

Community meals and banquets could include the avocados, grapes, egg dishes, breads, potatoes, etc., all free in a smorgasbord-supermarket manner. There is no such thing as money when the potato farmer goes to the blacksmith to repair his hoe. These jobs that people perform are thought of differently than the old fashioned jobs. There is a different driving force than to just make paper money. The driving force is wanting to do the tasks, fix the leaks, design the leak-proof, and make the city the best city possible. The better work today means less work tomorrow.

There are only a few hours needed to keep a balanced city running. The blacksmith may spend time fixing the hoe that supplies his potatoes, but can't complain when in the old system he would have to work eight hours a day. He gets the same rewards such as food, water, shelter, and materials to play with, so the motivation is still there to do one's part, but now with less time.

After a few hours of contributing to the society as a whole, citizens can spend the next few hours working on their own lives, homes, and chores to keep a daily balance.

After a noon break and a meal, this leaves half a day left over with plenty of free time. In a creative society, each person can spend the next few hours making creative things. There are no limits to how individuals may use this time.

The few hours after this can be used to work with others to create things like music, films, electronics, etc.. It's okay to mix up these last four hours into all collaborative or all working alone as long as you're being creative. After the evening meal comes the time to share with everyone else. Give the plays. Display your art. Show the movies. Show off your new electronic gizmos. Praise, be praised and be inspired by your fellow creators.

As a creative society makes more amazing creations, the rest of the world may pay with old fashioned money, but the city elders would trade that for actual, physical materials needed for more creations. Gold is the best metal for electronics so the elders would appreciate it for its usefulness rather than a dollar amount.

From here advanced humans aren't driven by greed for money, but for what they are doing in reality. The cities built show character, just as its citizens are all interesting creative characters, with their creative clothes, ornaments, and magical items.

Now you have people who instead of all being the same, and shunning those that are different, they now appreciate and embrace anything that's creative and new. The more different, the more colorful the world. The attitudes of yourselves, as pieces in this puzzle of creativity, reflect a complete freedom to be your happy selves as free individuals.

What happens when you find a domineering person in your face? Where will those that want to govern others be placed in a new system where freedom is the rule?

Chapter 13
GOVERNMENT

Now that humans have positive cities popping up and people governing themselves to have healthy lives and relationships, what happens to those individuals that have attachments to laws and how crimes are dealt with? There are many that insist murder should be handled this way, and thieves should be handled that way, yet this is dictating how people should act. But dictating that everyone handle situations in the same way stifles any chance of maturing past this point (like a world filled with only one type of old fashioned snowshoe.) The more people listen to their hearts and intellects, the more bad situations can be redirected to mature outcomes.

The advanced future may indeed have a system of officials, but there is a marked difference from past forms of government. This future structure of people that deal with laws, and man's struggle with doing good or bad, does not interfere with unlawful situations. This future structure simply notes how the situation was handled and has it nicely organized with all the other ways this situation was handled by others.

These buildings of government are now more like

libraries to be used for information and reference. If you or a township wants to deal with a thief, there is a library of suggestions collected from around the world, but the decision is up to you; and your decision, and outcome, will be documented. One person might catch the thief and harm him, while another might throw eggs at him until he runs away. Another might just give him a job picking avocados, thus feeding him so he doesn't have to steal ever again.

Now the world is filled with different people, tribes and townships dealing with smoothing out their own imbalances. If a man kills another man's wife, it will be that husband who reacts in the way of his nature. On one side of the planet a husband will kill the other, and that's the way it is. Elsewhere husbands deal with the guilty ones depending on their Aquaian or Pyroian levels.

The killer, or doer of the deed will just have to deal with the outcome, and if he has done something terrible to provoke another, then the repercussions may be severe. Now instead of a punishment being decided by a council, it will be the one that's wronged that will decide the outcome; but, now with the prime direction to find creative, non-destructive, non-regrettable solutions. To rise above the person that made the regrettable mistake.

These will be the tests of how far humans have conquered their Pyroian natures. As Aquaians mature and pass more of life's tests these scenarios will continue to be documented as reference for others.

An Old Scholar by Koninck Salomon (1609-1656)

There may be some barbaric consequences and also amazingly transcending good endings, but there will also be a respect for the world one finds one's self in.

Many people believe that without a government forcing people to be good, that chaotic and murderous scenarios would take over. This is not so when you break down what would cause such actions. If there was a lack of food then, yes, there would be a struggle to survive, but there is more than enough food. If there were crazy people running around, killing with no mercy, then you would struggle to survive, like in wartime. But when people are happy and healthy they would rather be a friend than attack you in a frustrated rage.

Most everyone wants peace. The vast majority of people are tired of the old ways and comprise the actual manpower needed to build your advanced societies. Most people, that do the actual work and keep the country running, are ready for a change. The question is if those operating on old Pyroian formulas are ready to give up the corrupting power, and explore a new Aquaian age.

Years ago the early civilizations liked to trade things. They had to travel across the desert to get back and forth. Humans started to dwell in the middle of the desert in order to catch the traders coming each way. These early humans were called the middle men. They would just sit and let the traders come to them. They would arrange trades between the traders asking only a portion in return for their troubles. They became fat because they let everyone else do the actual labor while they earned their share by using their minds.

There were always those that had things, and those that wanted things, but now trade was intercepted by the middle men. Now 10 oranges traded for 10 apples means the orange guy only gets 8 apples and the apple guy only gets 8 oranges. The middle man gets 2 apples and 2 oranges without ever having to climb a tree.

Soon the middle man would arrange to have 100 oranges left with him so that when the guy got there later with 100 apples the deal could be made. So middle men started writing certificates of debt for the orange guy to represent the 80 apples he was due. Money has always been like an I.O.U.. It's not a credit but a debt. Look at money and it even says "...for all debts, public and..."

As years went by there were more and more items being traded, middle men to help with the transfer, and more money to keep track of everything. The problem was the middle men not only became corrupt, but became more frustrated with their disconnection from life. It may have seemed smart to sit back while everyone else did the work, but being a part of the creative process is what brings happiness and fulfillment.

No one can rise above their mammalian natures. To join in the groups and accomplish projects is rewarding for the majority, but what about the middle man? Another aspect of a middle man, who had devoted himself to making money, and mental dealings, was that usually he wasn't very strong in the ways of the heart and emotions. These middle men became very cold and heartless. They had a hard time holding on to friendships. Their family lives were filled with frustration, arguing, and imbalance.

Part of the world, its individuals and governments process of moving into a healthy future, requires the middle men to also let go of the frustrating past, and help make the healthy future happen (not only on the outside but inside yourselves.) Although the old Pyroian mindset was to control and dictate, soon you'll see the new Aquaian mindset has got much deeper rewards.

Once the old routines of the middle men have been restructured and they are happy, healthy, and well balanced, they can then join the others in helping to raise the barn walls, or helping to put out barn fires. Learn to climb trees, pick fresh food, and how to make things. The smarter ones will help design more advanced transportation, bridges, buildings, water systems, and food systems. They will design without the corrupt mindset of someone in power, but with the creative mindset of someone that respects the world, and the power in their hands.

So a society or government is really nothing more than the people that comprise it. When each of you govern your own lives, the bigger whole that you are a part of will become more balanced. So now that there are not such extreme forces dictating your life, how will you spend your day? All laws, rules, and financial burdens have been lifted, and you are now completely free. Now that others aren't telling you what to do, how will you handle the responsibilities of life? How will you behave yourself so as not to provoke others to harm you? How will you develop yourself, and how will you fit into the bigger puzzle, yet still be an individual?

Chapter 14
INDIVIDUALISM

So how would you as a person be a part of a larger whole, yet still be respected as an individual piece of that whole? There is the mind of the ant and the mind of the ant colony. Your individual self, in order to feel happy in life and satisfied, will have to be respected amongst your fellow creative humans.

Societies of the past would convince people to follow styles or economic paths which would lead to happiness. If a shoe brand was in style, everyone would wear it and those that didn't would be the target of peer-pressure techniques.

The mistake in this old formula is that to feel yourself as an individual accepted by others, you would have to conform to a status quo. This robotic mimicry of what's accepted by the world outside yourself is not fulfilling, and was only a technique in an economic system to get you to work more and buy more, using your inner need to be accepted and loved.

As societies mature, so will the ways you as an individual, can play your part in the bigger scheme of things, and also enjoy the warm feelings of acceptance.

Now, rather than spending the day conforming yourself, you instead explore your creative spirit and learn the magic behind creating things. Humans can make so many things, so let's use the cuckoo clock as an example. When your creative mind has advanced to the point that you're making the most amazing cuckoo clocks, with moving parts, lights, and sounds, then others will praise your creative level. It's these pats on the back that are the most genuine and fulfilling. It's not a blind acceptance of you in the club, but a wholehearted acceptance of you and your creative spirit.

Balanced cities will not just be simple, happy people living together without the old destructive ways, but instead will actually be designed around creative ways, and will accomplish things after all the wheels are turning together. The items coming out of a balanced city will be steps beyond what the rest of the old world has to offer so these treasured creations will be highly desired.

An example could be the electronics that evolve into such tantalizing gizmos that the rest of the world can't wait to trade them for their money. Things like phones and computers can keep evolving, and the most creative will be at the forefront. Less tangible creations like music, from the right creative people, can touch the hearts of the most frustrated of countries.

In the more balanced cities you'll find that the

common belief in creativity can unite individuals with a shared internal commonality. Two artists are very different, but in the creative spirit they are actually the same. There is no desire to fight or battle once acceptance has been reached.

Columbia and Britannia victory shake after the war by Sigismund Goetze (1921)

A creative society joins forces rather than fighting. They spend their day creating together. Remember, they don't think in terms of money; but in terms of trading for more materials to make more items, to deeper explore their creativity, and to symbolize the creative spirit that brings all humans peace, well-being, and happiness.

A balanced city can be made to be ultra-efficient. The transportation system can be designed to not need fuel. It can be designed as a huge roller-coaster system utilizing the slopes and gravity to propel the cars on tracks (that cuts fuel needs in half right there.) Once at the bottom of the city these cars can be pulled to the top by cables. These cables can be connected to large tanks of water, filled high above the city, so as when the heavy tanks descend down they pull the cars to the top. This water can be dumped into a water supply, above the city, so that the tanks can return for more water. This is a 100% gravity powered transportation system.

While designing the tubes that people travel in, attention can also be given to smaller tubes to move other items such as materials and food. Fiber-optics can carry free light throughout the city as well as carry images, information and entertainment.

While designing the water system to utilize the organic power of gravity, it's soon learned the water can power generators for free electricity. Solar and wind power produce only droplets of electricity, but the force of water produces enough power to make it worthwhile.

Old societies cut down the trees that covered everything to make way for solar panels. Then they used even larger amounts of electricity just trying to cool things down with air conditioners (making things even hotter outside.) Solar panels simply couldn't produce enough electricity to power the now needed air conditioners. Humans can avoid many of their extra electric needs by cooling things down the old fashioned way with trees. Photosynthesis is much more efficient than photoelectric. Solar panels just can't measure up to leaves.

Trees can create cool shade beneath, but so can living underground. Caves have been found to be cool in the hottest environments. They stay the same temperature whether it's hot or cold above. Once the cement has dried, a balanced city is covered over with Earth. A forest/jungle is encouraged to grow above the city and only minimal portals connect the interior with the exterior, both above and below, for natural air flow.

The reason for this is the old cities of the past had to knock nature out to make room for their dwellings. People enjoyed their private, secure worlds inside, but when they went outside, the view of their world was the exterior of buildings and other man-made items. They lacked nature, so when designing a balanced city the exterior is as full of plants and animals as possible.

People will always want their safe, man-made boxes to nest in. But now when you venture out, you can enjoy real nature, which helps harmonize your mental world with your real physical world.

When designing the rows of buildings they can follow the design of slopes and rolling hills so that between could be valleys. The valleys could have streams to encourage the wild life, for food irrigation, and to make the experience more enjoyable for city inhabitants when they spend time outside. Designing a city to utilize gravity and water power is not difficult.

A balanced city would be strategically safe from attack, not only because it is a large bomb shelter, but safety is built into the design. The city parameter will be protected by more advanced gizmos, machinery, and electronics. The risk of attack can be prepared for, and the citizens can enjoy safety with out becoming soldiers.

When the stresses of life have melted away and the citizens can get down to creating things to trade to the world, there will be no end to the momentum once started. The better and more advanced items may shift the world market. Things from a balanced city can be the best there are and can represent prestige.

The richer a creative city becomes, the less it is worth invading. As much as another country might want what the balanced city has, it can't steal it. They can't run in and kill everyone to gain power. What makes the balanced city so desirable is the creative mindset that drives its citizens. Any country that wants this doesn't have to go to war to get it. They can restructure the blueprints of their own societies so that their own people can advance in their creative endeavors.

When a society lets go of the old ways, and boldly redesigns itself from scratch using the power of creativity, you will see humans mature into the balanced beings Earth can be proud of. The old cities pushed humans to set aside their morals in order to survive, and they did unspeakable acts for basics like food, water, and shelter.

Fruit Seller (Oil on canvas) by Vincenzo Campi (1580)

An individual living in a balanced city is not stressing about food, water, shelter, or survival; these basic human needs are built into the balance. The stresses of survival are non-existent, and so is the crime found in old, barbaric societies. What occupies the happy citizen's mind are ways to enrich one's creative spirit.

The entertainment they make, and watch, will also be different. A study showed that people emulate what they see. A bunch of children were shown a film where a room is full of toys and a child hits a clown doll on the head with a hammer. After the film each child was put into the same room filled with toys and each child found the hammer and hit the clown doll on the head. Out of all the toys they picked the ones seen in the film and then emulated what they had seen.

Knowing that humans emulate the visuals poured into their heads makes more reasons to make those visuals what you do want and not what you don't want. The old form of entertainment was very barbaric, destructive and negative. The new form of entertainment is harmonious, constructive and positive; more Aquaian.

Feeling power in life now is not over others, but over oneself. The more different the person or their creations are, the more they adhere to, and are accepted by, the common belief system of creativity. This belief system unites humans. It is also filled with acceptance, encouragement, and praise.

Happiness for humans is not that complicated when you study what makes other mammals have happy lives. Yes, not only other animals but especially, other mammals, can teach you a lot.

Chapter 15
MAMMALS

There are many humans that offer advice for a fulfilling life, but you will learn more from the other mammals around you. As a mammal you truly want to get along with others. It's built into the pack animal attitude. The reason for this is mammal babies need their mothers to survive. Babies rely on breastfeeding for nourishment. This is what makes an animal a mammal. The fact that it has breasts means it is an animal with mammaries. Humans are classified using a combination of the words, mammary and animal. A mammary animal or, mammal.

There are a lot of other mammals to study and you'll quickly learn that humans have the same set of traits found in all these animals that breastfeed their children.

Because mammal babies are raised by others, they get used to family groups. A mother can instill a lot of peace and well-being in an innocent one. Human adults can forget how important nurturing feelings can balance one's soul, but a baby lives it every day. When humans got cocky and made themselves the smartest thing on the planet, they actually considered animals and plants lower beings (although the other mammals were further ahead in ways such as working in families, devotion, love, and raising their young properly.)

Mammals were persecuted, disrespected and even had their sex organs removed so they couldn't continue their bloodlines. The excuse was there was too many but in reality the majority of landlords didn't allow pets. The problem wasn't the natural act of giving birth but the unnatural absence of animal friends allowed in homes and lives. The solution was not to kill them or keeping them from being born but instead to live together as all animals do in nature. Despite all the money paid for rent, without animal friends the home is just a sterile box. Kids raised in sterile boxes, with only plastic toys, lack reality. All that money should equal a happy home.

People finally stood up for themselves and demanded natural rights allowing them to bring plants and animals back into their man-made worlds. Which meant children could once again watch how a mother cat takes care of her kittens. The ways the kittens sleep together in a clump. The ways they play and learn. The devotion the mother has along with concern, love, and nurturing. She teaches them things by simply doing them herself. She's smart enough to know the little ones emulate and copy her.

When one sees a happy mother cat curled up with

her babies, it's easy to see the peace and well-being humans also strive for. Deep down humans want everything to be okay. You enjoy the safety of the den; it's like the safety of the womb. When the kittens are all playing together, their bright eyes remind humans of how exhilarating life can be once a safe environment is obtained. This is the happiness humans seek.

Because you laid your head at your mother's heartbeat and enjoyed this nurturing closeness, nothing has changed now that you're an adult. Humans are dealt many frustrating and traumatic events that would overwhelm the mind, yet your nerves can be calmed by a simple, nurturing hug from a loved one.

The old economic societies alienated people from each other, and relationships between family and friends were far from harmonious. The old ways convinced people their happiness would come from making money or buying products.

As mammals, you can never be happy if you don't have harmony with your family and friends. No amount of money can change this. Selfishness will make it harder. If there is frustration and anger in your inter-personal relationships, that is part of who you are. Even if you pretend to be on top of things, you are truly out of balance in yourself, and the world outside yourself.

It's worse if you lie to yourself and avoid the truth. Is

it worth it to you? If peace, well-being, and happiness rely on a balance with those around you, how many in your life can you consider a loved one? One that truly cares about you, loves you, and would nurture you back to health? Are they amazed at the things you do in life? Do they praise and encourage your amazing self? Would they save you if you were drowning?

In a balanced city, you would be rich in friends and loved ones. The old concepts of collecting money never did lead to happiness, yet when you find yourself in a group of others, working on projects, you notice how great you feel. The camaraderie between individuals in a group creates an atmosphere conducive to harmony. It feels good. Take an acting class and you'll notice it's more than fun during the rehearsals as you all plan, prepare and perfect the creation you are all a part of.

This creative process brings people closer. When the group is comfortable and balanced you can lose yourself in how great it feels. Like when all the electrons, protons, and nucleus fall into place, because while in orchestrated orbits, it just feels so good. Like tastes and flavors can entice you to eat, orgasms can entice you to procreate. All matter that humbly gives itself to Earth's nurturing, creative spirit gets to feel good.

Elation is a wonderful example of the many emotions humans can feel. When you study other mammals you'll notice they can be curious, upset, loving, concerned, humorous and also can feel great.

Nursing Her Child (Oil on canvas) by Mary Cassatt Louise (1896)

You'll also notice that all breastfeeding animals go through an awkward stage of getting to know new beings. Feeling odd, scared or shy at first. They play it safe while quietly learning. Timidness eventually turns to the comfortability stage and then the fun begins.

As much fun as they can have, they are also

psychologically brittle, and can become very depressed. There are a lot of sad examples of what other mammals go through emotionally, and some of you can attest that mental pain can be overwhelming.

Many have learned about the baby chimpanzees that were given only a wire mother to cling to and they died. The wire mother was covered in a soft towel and the next round of baby chimpanzees survived, but with psychological defects. Quite a difference to a healthy baby chimpanzee hanging onto its real mother, and how it matures into healthy adult life.

Humans are not any different. Just as you found peace and well-being while held at your mother's chest, there still is the need to sometimes be held or hugged. The heart and body put out slow, relaxing rhythms (while the Sun puts out quicker frequencies which excessively vibrate, agitate and shake up your nerves.) You've been raised in safety, held against your mother's mellow heartbeat (rhythms that console, relax and bring peace,) and everything was okay. It sounds simple because it is simple. Make sure you have closeness in your life and you will be a happy human.

When your mammalian needs are taken care of you will feel happy, emotionally balanced, and have the confidence to go deeper into this amazing, creative world. Nothing can hold you back. You are truly free.

Chapter 16
FREEDOM

We've expounded on the topic of all your Free Time and we've arrived at the topic of Freedom. Take some free time to discuss the concept of freedom with others and you'll notice something. Most everyone can spend hours telling you what they don't like about the world, and these things can be broken down into every detail and perfect logic.

A lot of brain power goes into thoughts about a disharmonious world where pollution is stifling life, oxygen producing trees are wiped out, varieties of animal life are decreasing, racism, sexism, and basically a whole slew of things that humans are doing wrong.

You could fill books with all the complaints of why humans were not free, but not many people actually created how they would live if they were indeed free. They just compiled complaints about oppression, tyranny, and lack of freedom.

These are valid topics, but they are only stepping stones to a better logic. Each sentence is negative and only contains what you don't want; it mentions nothing about what you do want. You would have found yourselves at the cookie jar again. Remember that when the brain gets a thought such as "I do not accept oppression" the "NOT" is removed because in reality, you can do anything.

The mind will see the detailed idea not as something "not to do," but the instructions for something to do. What the head really heard was "go into the cookie jar" and in the last case, "I do --- accept oppression." Reword this to a positive, such as, "I accept the responsibilities of freedom."

Ponder this positive rewording for awhile, and soon you will see what an effect words and ideas have on the brain. Create a special voice that jumps out when you hear or think something negative. It can remind you to reformulate the idea or sentence into a more positive form before it can be digested properly.

You can catch yourself when you get to a cookie jar scenario such as "I do not like pollution" and rearrange the idea to more of what you do want, "I like a clean and healthy environment." Now the idea is ready to store. Soon, one by one, each idea is rearranged before storing, and a stockpile of positive ideas will begin to surface into the real physical world. A stockpile not of what you don't like, but of what you do like.

For some of the other ideas you've not yet stored properly, you might come up with such prose as: "Trees are amazing forms of life that I respect, protect and nurture." "The many varieties of animals make life in this paradise interesting, and are very precious examples of Earth's creativity." "Humans are the same in that they all have differences, from skin color and freckle placements to faces and personalities." "I like fresh air and water so all beings can live healthy and thrive."

If you think about oppression all day then that is what you'll get. The more you think about the things that you really do want, the better your chances of actually obtaining what you want. If you want a healthy life with friends, activities, freedom, and an all around world of harmony, then that is what you must think about. You must see the target before you can expect to hit it.

Your entertainment will also have to mature so that it is filled with what you do want and not what you don't want. Rather than filling your heads with Pyroian scenarios the imagery will be Aquaian scenarios.

While you still have a chance, you must create a paradise before the power, as usual, falls into the next hands. If the Sun does win its power game, humans will certainly feel foolish standing there on ground that is melting all around into a molten, fiery hell. You'll wish you had this second chance; a chance to embrace your Aquaian side and help create a water planet that can survive the fiery universe, self contained and powered like a giant balanced city to last forever.

Once humans have mastered their understanding of AquaPyro Dynamics, their creations, including their cities, will better incorporate the real physical world; so will their minds and perceptions of the world. A foundation to reality so the freed human creative spirits won't spin out of control as they did in the past.

The Pastoral State (Oil on canvas) by Thomas Cole (1836)

With your new freedom comes a new power and serious responsibility. You must now choose. Do you want to join the creative club, or the destructive club? Do you want to hate, or do you want to love? Would you prefer to be loved rather than hated? Do you want to be an Aquaian, or a Pyroian?

Chapter 17
AQUAIAN OR PYROIAN?

The Pyroian dynamics have outweighed the Aquaian dynamics for many years now; resulting in war, death, destruction, forcefulness, manipulation and domination.

So, it turns out the gods or higher beings aren't invisible. They have been the two biggest things right in front of you the whole time. They have been the two biggest players, on this stage of life, around you. They have been battling for millions of years (before humans were even invented.) An age old battle between fire and water, between creation and destruction.

The time has come, once and for all, to decide which will be the God to dedicate your life to. Should humans choose the old Fire-God and continue on the path to an Armageddon? To end this planet's life with fire and brimstone? To burn Her, and all Her magic? Or should humans choose the Water-Goddess, as the kind and nurturing queen, and follow her path to life forever?

If working for the Fire-God makes you a demon and working for the Water-Goddess makes you an angel, then which do you choose?

The old ways of dividing yourselves only caused

confusion and frustration, so now try uniting yourselves so you can think clearly, and then calmly make a good decision. Make the right choice without being deceived.

If you've been a Pyroian for most of your life and you're unsure if you can douse your fiery nature, then ask yourself why you try so hard to be a Pyroian? Isn't it because deep down you really are frustrated because you don't have the well-being all mammals require? As frustrated and sour as one can become, it's easy to mistakenly snap at those around you, and often it's a bad way of getting what will actually make you happy. Don't make things worse by spiraling into negativity.

Getting in touch with one's soul and speaking honestly, from the heart, can have better results than your old ways that pushed people away. Anyone can feel the pain of loneliness. Rather than inflicting pain on others, so they know how you feel, you'll see that friendliness can get you what you really need to feel in return. Life can be great. Life can feel good. Let your demons fall back into grace and become the original angels they started out as.

To explore your Aquaian side can not only be new, exciting, and adventurous, but it's an amazing feeling to get in touch with one's inner instincts. When a baby bird stretches and feels its body from the inside, soon it feels in touch with its inner instincts and it is ready to learn to fly. As you get better at feeling your Aquaian instincts you also will learn to soar through your creative world.

Although many Pyroians have never made anything and consider themselves not very artistic, there is a surprise that awaits. It sometimes takes a lot of pushing and moving forward with creative endeavors to get the momentum going, but if you're human then you definitely have creative potential; and you'll eventually amaze even yourself.

Bacchanale (Oil on canvas) by Paul Jean Gervais (1859-1936)

Once you embrace your Aquaian nature, you'll notice that water saturates many of the aspects in your life. Not only is this a water planet, but the seemingly solid life-forms running around everywhere are actually water-filled. Water is one of those magic spaces that connect things, but this is one that humans can see. Just as the fish maneuver around in the ocean, so do the birds maneuver in the air. Water and oxygen are only different because of a few molecules. They are almost the same.

Scientists have discovered the feathers on a bird are not a form of hair or nail, but a form of scale; the same scale found on fish, but elongated. Birds, fish, and humans learn to appreciate air and water. They're a part of life. They connect life both inside you and outside you. A lot of magic happens in between.

Just as water gives life, fire can take life. Should humans give life or take life? There are amazing things happening on this planet, and it would be wise to understand what they are rather than burning them.

Your Pyroian side can get too wound up to think straight, so let your Aquaian, intuitive self, sense what's best. When the Sun is down and you are about to sleep, you can pray for guidance. Contemplate this serious question, and let the Creator inside you answer.

For those still not sure if you would like to die in fire, or live with water, and which to vote for, then a simple test can help you decide. Think about which would feel better between putting your finger in; water or fire? You can do this in your mind, not in real life.

No one has to really put their finger in fire to know their choice. The Aquaian deep inside cries out to put the finger in the water.

It seems no one is 100% Pyroian. No one really wants to die burning in fire. The pain is much worse than a burned finger. If you don't want a fire planet then vote for a water planet. If you used to believe in destruction yet don't want to destroy yourself, then vote to re-create yourself. Choosing Earth over the Sun means you choose to be an Aquaian over a Pyroian. Vote to become a planet of Aquaians.

Finally, Aquaians can be free to nurse themselves and the water planet back to health. Vote for a water planet. Vote to praise Earth and shield her from the Sun's attacks. Fire and radiation are the Sun's weapons. Don't help the Sun by attacking life here from the inside. Don't betray Her but protect Her (just as She also protects you.) Let the plants lushly cover everything. Avoid nuclear power and strengthen your creative power. Vote against the fiery end and for the watery rebirth.

Once humans as a whole share the same prime direction and combine their efforts, you will see that anything is possible. When humans worship, love, and protect the planet, it will become natural to worship, love, and protect each other, and the other forms of life.

Now it's your turn. You get to choose. You get to vote. Fire or water? The Sun or Earth? Pyroian or Aquaian?

www.ingramcontent.com/pod-product-compliance
Lightning Source LLC
Chambersburg PA
CBHW060936040426
42445CB00011B/887